Ordinary Girl

Donna Summer

Ordinary Girl

THE JOURNEY

with Marc Eliot

Villard Ⓥ New York

VILLARD and "V" CIRCLED Design are registered
trademarks of Random House, Inc.

Library of Congress Cataloging-in-Publication Data
Summer, Donna.
Ordinary girl : the journey / by Donna Summer ;
with Marc Eliot.
p. cm.
ISBN 1-4000-6031-1
1. Summer, Donna.   2. Singers—United States—Biography.
I. Eliot, Marc.   II. Title.
ML420.S952A3 2003
782.42164'092—dc21   2003045026
[B]
Printed in the United States of America on acid-free paper
Villard website address: www.villard.com

2 4 6 8 9 7 5 3 1

First Edition
Book design by Mercedes Everett

In memory of my mother,
Mary Ellen Davis Gaines.

Bold and righteous, generous to a fault, giving without
taking, sacrificing much for me, suffered much through me,
never complaining, ever enduring.

I hope she's looking down . . .

My constant cheerleader throughout my life,
I love you and your dream has come true.

Release me from the past that I may be free to soar into the future.

—*Donna Summer*

Contents

1. Sacred Rain   3

2. As the Crow Flies   18

3. Touched by an Angel   41

4. Life on the Autobahn   54

5. Love in Vienna   71

6. Munich Madness   91

7. Love to Love You Baby   101

8. Stardom in America   117

9. Thank God It's Friday   142

10. Toot-Toot, Beep-Beep   164

11. Hard for the Money   180

12. The Connection   194

13. The Gift   207

14. Bringing Up Babies, and Parents, Too   223

Acknowledgments and Credits   249

Donna Summer Discography   253

Ordinary Girl

1

Sacred Rain

I have many wonderful childhood memories of growing up in an old cobblestoned neighborhood of Boston. In my mind I can still see the way it looked to me as a child. It was a mystical place filled with gas lamps and beautiful foliage. There were low-slung buildings styled in birthday-cake architecture and covered in climbing ivy, all of it reflecting colonial times. It was like growing up in a great big live-in diorama of the American Revolution, New England style.

I remember one haunting autumn afternoon when I was only five years old, standing by myself in the nearby courtyard of my little redbrick schoolhouse. All of a sudden I became acutely aware of my surroundings for the first time. The whooshing leaves, the gentle wind, and the uneven ground beneath my feet touched me in a profound way. The sensation overwhelmed me, all at once bringing me closer to and yet isolating me from everything. It was frightening to have my senses

Here I am at around three or four years of age with my sisters at the beach. Left to right: me, Linda, Amy . . . and cousin Barbara's legs.

Photo courtesy of the Gaines family

so abruptly awakened. In that moment I realized that everything in the schoolyard, in the streets, at home, *in the world* must
have been designed by someone, and that someone must be
God. I was humbled to my childish core. From that moment on
I knew I wanted to be connected to Him with all my heart and
soul.

I was born LaDonna Adrian Gaines on New Year's Eve,
December 31, 1948, into a loving family with deep spiritual
roots.

My daddy, Andrew Gaines, was the proverbial "son of a
preacher man." He was born in Fairfax, Alabama, where his father, Reverend Solomon Louis Gaines, was a Christian minister
of one of the biggest churches in the little town. Grandpa
Solomon died suddenly while sitting in church when Daddy
was only eight years old. Shortly thereafter, his mother, my
grandmother Eula, moved her three daughters and four sons to
Boston.

During World War II, my father fought in Germany as a
sergeant in the army. After discharge from the service, he returned to Boston, where he took any job that was available,
working as a butcher, a wallpaper hanger, and a television re-
pairman. During the late forties he met and fell in love with
Mary Ellen Davis, a green-eyed, curly-haired beauty from
Boston, the woman who was to become my mother.

My mother was a first-generation American, her parents
having emigrated from a small fishing village in Nova Scotia.
Although I've never quite been able to sort out the combination
of ingredients, I know my heritage is mixed, something like

5

African, Indian, and Dutch-Irish—all filtered down into one body: mine.

I have warm memories of my maternal grandmother, Annie Glouster, whom we used to call Nickel-Bag Annie. Whenever she would visit she would untie the handkerchief she'd stuffed with nickels and give each of us kids a shiny new one—thus the nickname. (She was the inspiration for a song I wrote years later called "Nickel-Bag Annie.") Back in those days "nickel bag" had a sole reference— to a bag of nickels.

My father was quite adept at fishing. It was a skill that came in handy after he married my mother. Whenever they ran short of cash, Daddy knew he could always bring home plenty of fresh food, enough to feed the entire house. And there were plenty of young mouths to feed—four, to be exact: Jeanette, the oldest; next, my brother, Ricky; then me; and Amy, the youngest at that time. I can remember many times when we ate fish for days at a time! No one ever complained about eating fish. We loved it!

My parents spent most of their waking hours trying to keep a roof over our heads. There was little time and little money for anything but the bare necessities. We rarely took trips anywhere, except for the occasional summer car ride to the amusement park. By and large, travel was restricted. My entire world was confined to places I could walk or take a bus to: school, church, the playground.

Even though we weren't dollar rich, we had something we thought was worth a lot more—a great neighborhood filled with wonderful people. The first few years of my life we lived in a low-income housing project that had been built after the Second World War. All types of people lived in our project: whites, blacks, Hawaiians, Asians, and others. It was a rare example of ethnic diversity.

Grandma Eula lived with us in our apartment. Both of my parents worked, so it was very convenient to have Grandma Eula around to take care of us.

One of my fondest childhood memories is of watching my parents dance. Mummy was very light on her feet, and let me tell you, Daddy was no slouch either! Whenever they did the lindy hop, which was often, he would grab my mother, fling her between his legs, roll her through, and hoist her in the air. All the kids would gather around whenever they danced their fast, twirling routines. Years later I wrote a song with my sisters called "Watchin' Daddy Dance," recalling those moments of spontaneous love that filled our home.

My mother was quite shapely and outstandingly pretty, with extraordinary light green eyes, a shade I've never seen on anyone else. Wow, what a face! Her great maternal instincts kept everyone together and happy. She knew when to say yes and when to say no, and whenever she was in doubt, she'd put all final decisions on the broad shoulders of my daddy. If I asked her for permission to do something she wasn't sure about, she'd subvert her own authority by saying, "Wait until your father comes home."

Not that she couldn't be a disciplinarian when she felt *that* necessity. In those days if you *didn't* give your children the occasional swat on the behind, it meant you *didn't* love them. As the comedian Chris Rock says, "I ain't sayin' that it was right . . . but I understand." My mother had no compunction about throwing the occasional hairbrush our way when we were being especially rambunctious. Needless to say, there were a lot of broken brushes in our house. But ultimately she loved to laugh more than anything else, because she preferred to see the humor in life's daily routines. On more than one occasion my ability to make her laugh saved my little brown behind a good butt whuppin'. Luckily, Daddy rarely spanked; however, his raised voice was even more torturous. He had a pair of lungs that could yell loud enough to make the pots and pans rattle in the kitchen, and that was something I dreaded even more than being spanked.

As a child, I had an innate moral compass, which was enhanced by my upbringing. Whenever I did something my parents would think was wrong, I would know it long before they'd say so and feel completely awful. I'd put myself through the dreadful anticipation of "waiting for Daddy to come home." Believe me, that waiting was as bad for me as the actual moment of his arrival.

When I was still a very small child my mother used to love to braid my hair. She had extraordinarily agile fingers and could gather together as few as four strands of hair at a time, which made for a very long period of time that I had to sit still. You could be bald and she could *still* braid your hair! The problem for me was that I didn't really like the way I looked with my hair braided. She braided my hair so tight it made my eyes slant. I'd see myself in the mirror afterward and wonder who was that little girl staring back at me. Being braided and not liking it was one source of my low self-esteem. I'm sure many girls of color know exactly what I'm talking about and will completely understand. The first thing I did when I became successful was to invest in lots of fashionable wigs.

✳

One Friday afternoon, just before sundown, I was walking home from the playground with a couple of school friends when one of them said, "Hey, I bet I can beat you home." I bet them they couldn't. Without saying a word, they both took off running. At almost the same time, I heard someone calling from a nearby building. I quickly turned my face in the direction of the voice.

Pow!!! Smack in the forehead!!! I didn't know what hit me. I fell to the ground. My friends were gone, having run away. At first I didn't know where I was or who I was, for that matter. I crawled on the ground in a circle, too stunned to even cry. I didn't feel any pain. I was unquestionably in shock. I lay down again, but when I opened my eyes, it was dark. The sun had gone down and I couldn't remember how to get home. Talk about a traumatic experience for a young child!

I managed to get to my knees when I heard my brother's voice calling, "Donna Adrian Gaines!" I felt his hand on my waist pulling me up. "Get on my back," he said, recognizing that something was wrong. It was then that I started to cry. I began to realize that something bad had happened. My brother carried me into the light. I touched my face to wipe off what I thought were tears. My brother began to yell, "Oh my God, what happened to you!" I was covered in blood. I had been shot above the eye with some kind of cap gun or small-caliber gun, which had made a hole above my right eye.

My grandmother heard my brother screaming and ran out to see what had happened. I was rushed to the emergency room, where the doctors said, after a thorough examination, that I would recover.

Thank God for my brother. Shortly after this incident and several others involving my siblings, my mother and father decided to look for a safer environment for us.

＊

When I was six years old, my parents moved us out of the projects. We moved into a gray-and-white three-family Victorian house just outside Brookline. My parents, keenly aware that we were a black family living in a partially integrated middle-class neighborhood, wanted to make sure their children set a good example. We had to be neater and more polite than all the other neighborhood kids. God forbid we did anything vulgar. I remember getting a spanking from my father one time for wearing red fingernail polish, because in his opinion, the *only* ladies who wore that kind of adornment were hookers.

While my parents never mentioned our color as any kind of an obstacle, we were always encouraged to do our best, and to fit seamlessly into our community. We were never to give anyone an excuse for saying, "See? You just can't allow them to . . ." You can fill in the rest.

Our house at 16 Parker Hill Avenue had a huge backyard (or at least it seemed so at the time) and more room for us to move around. My aunt Mary and uncle George moved into the first floor with their growing brood; our family of six (Mummy, Daddy, and now four kids) occupied the second; and Grandma Eula lived on the third with two of our cousins whose parents were deceased. In addition, Mummy made our house welcome to all the neighborhood kids and wanted all of us to learn to be kind and to share whatever we had with others.

As a result, our house was always noisy and full of life. I must say there were many times when I was confused by it all. It was inside that confusion and chaos that I ultimately discerned my voice. Sometimes it seemed as if I were looking at life from underwater, a perspective that I gleaned as an eight-year-old girl from a real experience.

On one especially hot day during the summer, my brother, Ricky, took all of us to Brighton Pool. Sitting on the lip of the pool with Ricky, I asked, "How can I get to the other side?" He turned to me and said, "The best way to go from one side of the pool to the other is to simply walk across the bottom. The trick is to keep jumping up and down."

I was always the type to dive into things, literally and figuratively, regardless of whether or not I fully knew what I was getting into. I was about to learn what people meant when they warned against getting in over one's head!

I was only four feet eight inches at the time, and, sure enough, as I got nearer to the middle of the pool I found myself in well over my head. I kept jumping as Ricky had instructed;

however, each time I hit the bottom of the pool, I had more and more difficulty coming back to the surface. I realized I was drowning and I started to panic. Just then I saw a couple of young boys dive into the pool right over my head. I thought they would know I was drowning if I could only grab one of their legs. With all the strength I had left in me, I grabbed, but water filled my lungs and I blacked out.

I have no idea how long I was unconscious, but somehow I came to and found myself walking along the bottom of the pool toward the shallow end. I kept walking across the bottom of the pool, no longer in a state of panic, but rather in a state of peace. I walked until the water receded across my face. Looking up, I opened my eyes and saw the beautiful blue sky. My first thought was "Heaven is so beautiful. Why was I so afraid to die?" The emergency bell rang, jerking me back into reality. My sisters and brother jumped into the pool and pulled me out.

To this day I think of my near drowning as a baptism. Although I had no idea how I miraculously survived, I knew God was watching over me. From that moment on, it was a matter of faith to me that He would continue to watch over me and that He must have something special in mind for me. I had no idea what the future would be, but somehow I knew it would be something wonderful.

*

That year, 1956, was indeed a year of change. Nearly drowning adjusted my sense of purpose, and I seemed endued with a new sense of creativity. I was already into all kinds of music, espe-

cially the gospel music that was played and sung at the Grant
A.M.E. Church at 1900 Washington Street, a two-bus journey
from our house. I usually didn't take the second bus, as it was
only about a ten-minute walk from there. I enjoyed having that
time for myself, singing as I walked along to church. Often I'd
struggle to reach the high notes. One day I prayed and asked,
"God, please teach me how to sing better." I began to practice
my breath control.

During afternoons when I was alone in the house, I'd lie on
my stomach across my parents' bed and hold my breath to make
my diaphragm stronger. At first I could do it for only about fifteen seconds, but after a couple of weeks I was able to extend the
time to well over a minute. My mother was impressed by my
discipline.

Thank God for my mother's encouragement. "Do this
song" or "Do that song," she'd say. I loved singing for her because it seemed to make her so happy. My father was a fan as
well, especially when I learned to do impersonations of his favorite singers. He'd take me into the living room to listen to his
Brook Benton and Dinah Washington records and then make
me sing just like them. My father's favorite song was "What a
Difference a Day Makes," by Dinah, and it didn't take me very
long before I could mimic her down to her last dentalized *t*! I'd
sing it for him over and over. He loved it! Whenever my parents
had company, my sisters, Amy and Linda, and I would sing.
Everyone would just go crazy. "We've Come This Far by Faith"
was one gospel song we often sang. It was great having so much
music in our house.

This is the church I attended growing up in Boston. It's where I first sang publicly.
Photo courtesy of the Sudano family archives

My sisters and I didn't need much outside entertainment. We were more than willing to provide our own and share it with the world. All the kids who lived in our little neighborhood were like Spanky's Gang, and the Gaines girls were their personal entertainment. Even their parents were part of our original fan club. My mother used to tell me, If you have a gift, you have to share it, and whatever you share will come back to you thirty-, sixty-, even a hundredfold. We shared our gift of singing with anyone who would listen.

There was a nursing home next to our house. When we'd put on our backyard shows the elderly people in the home would stick their heads out of their windows and yell, "Come to the front porch so we can hear and see you better." They would request their favorite songs, and we would oblige with a little bit of everything, from gospel songs like "Amazing Grace" to old Irish ditties like "Danny Boy."

By the time I was twelve I was singing songs by the Supremes—of course, I *always* had to be Di-*ana*. I even had a special, lip-curling way of doing my main man, Elvis! *And* Connie Francis! I loved doing her "Lipstick on Your Collar." I'd sing that one with all the conviction I could muster. And I memorized everything that Dionne Warwick had recorded.

I never had any formal voice training as a child. I never took lessons, practiced notes, or sang scales. But when I'd open up and let my voice ring out, people said they could hear me all over the neighborhood. One time, my father swore, he was filling his car with gas several blocks away and he could hear me singing. And you know, I think he could!

I loved the excitement, the energy, and the attention our neighborhood shows provided, but every so often I felt the need to get away and be by myself. Living in a house with so many people made that very difficult. Sometimes I would do what I called my "hiding thing," where I would go into a closet, close the door, and simply enjoy the quiet or cry for no reason.

Other times I'd go for a walk by myself and find a place where I could just sit alone and daydream, daydream, daydream. My secret rituals kept me sane and grounded during those early years. I mastered the art of mentally flying.

∗

One fateful day, the soloist for our church choir unexpectedly fell ill. When it turned out there was nobody to cover for her, my mother volunteered me for the job. She convinced the powers that be that I was good enough to sing. They must have been desperate! Much to everyone's surprise—except my mother's—when I opened my mouth to sing the first song, "I Found the Answer, I Learned to Pray," a powerful and pure voice came out of me. My voice traveled all the way to the back of the church, cascading over the parishioners in attendance. It felt like sacred rain.

I'd had no idea I was going to sound that good! My mother and sisters started crying, along with the minister, which really scared me. Then, once again, the feeling came over me that I'd had in the schoolyard and also after my near-drowning experience, a sense of elation and suspension. Only this time, I could hear God's voice clearly and distinctly inside my head, saying,

"You're going to be famous. That's power, and you are never to misuse it."

It was a scary and wonderful moment. Only a few minutes earlier I'd been an ordinary girl about to sing before the neighborhood congregation. And then I'd heard these two incredible voices: first, my own, and then God's, setting me on the path of my life's journey.

2

As the Crow Flies

I sang regularly in the children's choir until I was old enough to graduate to the young adults' choir. Along the way I occasionally did some solo performing. I formed my first real group when I was fourteen years old, a trio with twin brothers, John and Earl. Later we added another girl and became a quartet. We'd sing for the neighborhood churches. We sang for the experience and not for any money, as I would not accept payment for singing for the One who had given me my voice. We had a great time.

I sang with the Lawrence Bagwell Choir for a while, and the glee club at Jeremiah E. Burke High. If I hadn't been able to sing, I surely would have dropped out of school. I also joined another group, called the Young Adults, a dancing-and-singing troupe that played around Boston. I wanted to knock on every door that had anything to do with music.

In spite of my singing ability, I grew up feeling very insecure. I was surrounded by my brother and sisters, who were constantly vying for the love of our parents. In my opinion, they were doing a better job of earning affection than I was. I felt inferior, a feeling which magnified my belief that I was ugly.

I had felt ugly ever since the age of seven, when I'd accidentally cut a three-inch gash in my face, along my right cheek. My father, who was always handy with tools and fixing things around the house, was refinishing our kitchen chairs and had taken the backs off their posts. I was trying to help out and bent down to wipe one of the chairs off. As I did so, I felt a sharp stabbing on the side of my face. Without realizing it, I'd caught myself on the razor-sharp tip of one of the exposed metal posts and had succeeded in slicing my right cheek wide open!

Daddy swooped me up, ran out of the house, put me in the backseat of his car, and rushed me to the emergency room of the neighborhood hospital. The doctors who treated me were afraid to use stitches on my cheek because they thought it would make whatever scar I was surely going to have even worse. Instead, they decided to tape my cheek back together. For months after, the wound just kept opening and oozing blood. Every time I smiled or even if I moved my head too quickly, the cut would start bleeding again. I became so self-conscious I dreaded anyone seeing me. I stayed in the house. For weeks I didn't attend school. I was so afraid that I would see somebody I knew, and they would see how ugly I had become.

Because of all the natural physical stress on that part of my face, the wound never did heal properly. It left a permanent scar that soon became an emotional one as well. The scar on my

Left to right: cousin Sheila, me in the back looking buzzed out on birthday cake, Bobby, and Amy in the foreground, in the very chair upon which I cut my face.

Photo courtesy of the Sudano family archives

cheek became the focal point for everything I hated about my-self. I was convinced that I had ruined myself for life and would never be attractive to anyone, especially a man. Every time I looked in the mirror, all I could see was that scar staring back at me, mocking me, and making me feel unworthy.

These feelings stayed with me a long time. For years I suf-fered from bouts of depression, and I wet my bed regularly. That was the last straw for my parents, who'd put up with my weird behavior in hopes that I would somehow grow out of it on my own. Once I became a bed wetter, my parents decided my problems were too serious to ignore any longer and they sent me to see a child psychiatrist.

Having a full house didn't help my fragile ego. My brothers and sisters were often cruel, calling each other all kinds of names, as only siblings can. They'd point their fingers and call me Scarface, Peanuthead, and Ducky. Now, of course, I can see they were trying to be affectionate, just having kid fun at my ex-pense. It was just my family's way.

As if being called names by my own family wasn't enough, a girlfriend's dad went so far as to call me Donna Ugly when-ever he saw me. Can you imagine an adult talking to a child like that? I heard these painful words "Donna Ugly, Donna, Donna Ugly" echoing in my head for years and years to come.

That's why to this day there aren't a lot of informal, un-posed photos of me around. Whenever anyone would take out a camera, I'd quickly hide, or make some funny face.

As a teenager, I tried hiding the scar on my face by wearing wigs. Once, a friend lent me a red hooker wig, which I secretly

Left to right: My mother, Mary, with cousin Sheila, me, and cousin Bobby on Parker Hill Avenue. I'm making faces again.

Photo courtesy of the Sudano family archives

intended to wear to school. However, on the way to school, my oldest sister, "the Boss," spotted me from behind. Without warning and in front of all my friends, she reached up and snatched that wig right off my head. Mortified, I grabbed my head and started screaming at the top of my lungs, "I'LL NEVER GO WITHOUT PINS AGAIN!" All of my friends fell over laughing at my expense. Jeanette and I reminisce and laugh about that wig every time we get together.

As a way of compensating for my perceived unattractiveness, I became a neat freak. If the house needed straightening, I'd drop whatever I was doing and fix everything up. If my parents' bedroom looked a little drab, I'd rearrange all the furniture in it. It was my way of imposing a sense of idealized order on the external world, in which I felt I could never truly fit. It was part of my need to make whatever things I could control look as beautiful as possible.

Mummy understood my sensitivity to the aesthetic and appreciated my need to create an attractive environment. My sisters and brother, on the other hand, didn't understand. They just thought I was being spoiled by my mother, who never tried to stop me from my self-appointed role as a would-be interior decorator.

My low self-esteem had both positive and negative effects. On the plus side, I worked especially hard to develop my sense of humor and my character, figuring if I wasn't going to be beautiful at least I could be the girl at the party with the great personality. On the minus side, try as I might, I could not control my bed-wetting.

One of our annual Easter family portraits. This one was taken when I was approximately twelve years old. Left to right: Sheila, my sister Linda, and me. *Photo courtesy of the Gaines family*

Even though my father knew it wasn't my fault, he would still punish me in some way. I knew my father loved me, in spite of his frustration with me. Somehow he believed that my bed-wetting was an act of defiance. (Unconsciously it may have been, in some way.) The doctor told him it was an emotional as well as a physical problem.

As children, we deal with a lot of things in unusual ways, things that leave us feeling ashamed, things that convince us there really is something "wrong." These things feed right into and reinforce whatever sense of low self-esteem is already there. For me, my bed-wetting and my father's reaction to it made me feel that I was inferior. I was very humiliated by this problem.

After seeing a psychiatrist, I was finally able to overcome bed-wetting at the age of sixteen. I realized that God must have allowed this obstacle in my path to help me find the strength and the belief in Him as well as in myself to overcome my shortcomings. However, to this day, the thought of being far from a ladies' room makes me shudder.

✳

My next step forward came when I found the courage to pursue singing as my life's work. This part of the journey began with a few tentative footsteps along the Boston Common.

I used to love to walk alone up Tremont Street in Boston by the old graveyards and look at all the headstones. One day when I was seventeen, as I was taking one of these walks, I heard some music floating in the air. Good music.

There was a lot of positive energy in this part of the city, the epicenter of what was then becoming the Boston music scene. The streets in and around Boston and Cambridge were packed with new clubs, one after the other, with wonderfully eclectic names like the Psychedelic Supermarket and the Boston Tea Party and Club 47. These were the key venues where everyone who was anyone simply had to play. Up-and-coming stars like Janis Joplin, the Chambers Brothers, and the Jefferson Airplane played these clubs. I used to peek into the windows and marvel at all the psychedelic lights and wild girls dancing in go-go cages, hoping to see one of these famous performers.

I still hadn't actually been inside any of these clubs—I was only seventeen years old and too young to be admitted. Nevertheless, the flow of youthful energy that poured out of these clubs was pervasive and ignited everyone under the age of twenty.

I was intrigued by the whole burgeoning sixties scene, so when I heard music while walking that day it seemed the perfect soundtrack to my own innermost thoughts. I was drawn to it, wanting to know where it was coming from, and who was making it. I decided to follow the trail of notes. It didn't take me long to discover that the music was emanating from one of the nearby buildings.

I figured it was some kind of school for musicians. Maybe I could find a coach in there and take some piano lessons or something. I went in the front door, walked up the stairs, and knocked on the door where the sound was coming from. Someone yelled, "Come in." I did and saw six college-age white guys with wild hair, sloppy clothes, and musical instruments who were in the middle of rehearsing. It was all so perfectly strange. "I fit right in," I thought.

One of them casually asked me if I was there for the audition. I didn't know what they were talking about, but I said, "Uh, yeah, sure, of course, that's exactly why I'm here." "Can you sing?" they asked. I didn't have to be asked that twice, and I broke right into my best Aretha Franklin, with a little "R.E.S.P.E.C.T." for all I was worth. I was singing without a mike, yet my voice could clearly be heard above their amplified instruments. I had found my place.

When I finished they all clapped and told me how much they loved the way I sang, and I was thrilled. They then told me they were really looking for a male lead. I left my number with them in case they changed their minds, or just needed someone to sing backup. I told them they shouldn't hesitate to call. Disheartened, I made my quick good-byes and left. I'd gotten only as far as the top of the stairs when a couple of the guys stuck their heads out the door and yelled, "Hey, could you, like, come back here? We talked it over and decided we want you to sing with us after all."

Cool! I went back inside and sang one of their original songs. It was obvious to all of us that we had an immediate and dynamic synergy. I seemed to blend naturally into the mix, as if we'd been performing together for years rather than minutes. Like, groovy, man.

"Hey, I'm in a rock 'n' roll band!" I yelled. We called ourselves the Crow. Hoby Cook did most of our songwriting, played the organ and electric piano, and was the leader of the band. The band also included Roger Schon on lead guitar, Mark Gould on trumpet, Steven Schrell on alto sax and flute, Joel Franklin on drums, and Vern Miller on bass and occasionally, if you can believe it, the tuba. Hoby had modeled the Crow after the band Blood, Sweat and Tears. The boys had been playing locally for a while and had gotten good enough to where they thought that with the right singer they might be able to take themselves to the next level.

Hoby was tall and good-looking. I liked him from the moment I laid eyes on him. He looked like a pirate to me, very handsome with dirty blond hair and a beard like Errol Flynn had in those old Hollywood swashbuckler films. Beyond the physical, though, I was drawn to his kindness. I liked the fact that he was the type of person who seemed to always want to please others and help people in any way he could. I identified with that.

He was a natural leader as well, and once I'd joined the band, he immediately took it upon himself to mold me into his vision. He began to shape my "look" so that I could fit in with the rest of the band. In other words, he became Professor Henry Higgins to my Eliza Doolittle.

I found my instruction under Hoby far more educational, not to mention enjoyable, than regular school. I'd been bored nearly to death with my classes for a long time and had felt like I was suffocating in school. With Hoby, learning took on a whole other kind of meaning.

Over the next several months, Hoby's contribution to my growth was immeasurable. He was my mentor in every way. He not only championed my singing talent but, even more importantly, bolstered my always tenuous self-esteem, trying everything he could to convince me that I was as special as he thought I really was.

For instance, he loved to take me out shopping, and always wound up buying me the kinds of things I could only dream of getting for myself but could never afford. One time he took me to a fancy jewelry store and bought me a pair of expensive, handmade gold earrings that had come from San Francisco's Haight-Ashbury district, which I thought was so great! He paid careful attention to the way I looked. My hair was longish at the time, the way a lot of girls in the neighborhood wore theirs. Hoby told me to cut it short, in the style of the big-eyed British model Twiggy, who was all the rage back then. He bought me beautiful clothes, dressing me in very expensive brocade Nehru jackets and bell-bottom pants. Even my mother got caught up in my makeover, filling out my wardrobe with a few new dresses she thought would please Hoby.

As you might imagine, all of this was so exciting to me! I felt for the first time as if I might actually go somewhere with my music. Music was my "first talent," the thing I loved to do at my happiest, or my most depressed. However, I wanted singing to be the means to other opportunities.

I wanted to use my singing as a springboard to what had secretly become my new career goal: becoming a movie actress. I had lately come under the spell of the silver screen. My plan was to be like Judy Garland and sing my way to a place that opened other doors.

I'd gone so far as to do some local community theater work,

but back then there weren't many doors open to black actresses, and I didn't want to play only "nanny" roles! I also knew I didn't look like Dorothy Dandridge or Lena Horne, which is what it took to break into the all-white world of Hollywood. So singing was to be my entrée.

Although he didn't know my private ambitions, Hoby sensed early on that I was serious about making it, and he was as eager as I was to turn my dreams into reality.

I suppose it was inevitable we would be intensely attracted to each other. We were opposites in every way, and yet that only seemed to heighten our attraction to each other. Hoby was from a very wealthy family but, I suspected, maybe not one with a whole lot of love. In that sense, I was far richer than he was. He had a strong need for love, and I had an equally strong need for approval. It seemed we were perfectly suited to give each other exactly what we needed.

Even though I was still underage, Hoby was able to get me into clubs, which is how I finally got to see some of those famous acts I'd only heard on the radio. Hoby wanted me to see exactly what it was about them that had made them so successful.

We spent a lot of time alone as well. We were young and playful and enjoyed each other's company. One time I decided to perm all that lovely hair of his. His hair came out all lush and curly, and he loved it! Up until then we had been very careful about our emotional demonstration, which is to say that we didn't have a physical relationship, but that night we could no longer avoid the obvious, and he kissed me full on the lips. It was the first time I had ever been kissed like that. *And I loved it!*

Here I am, approximately seventeen years old, going to the prom of a friend. *Photo courtesy of the Sudano family archives*

Hoby continued to educate me, always making sure to take me to all the nicest places in town, to all those fancy restaurants I could never otherwise have afforded. He showed me the proper way to eat, how to use all the different knives and forks. At the exclusive French restaurant Du Barry, Hoby introduced me to the hitherto unknown delights of escargot. He knew enough not to tell me that escargot were actually snails. When I was a kid I used to step on snails and then torture them by pouring salt on them. (I know, it's pretty sick.) I would never have knowingly put one in my mouth. *But, oh, that butter-and-garlic sauce! Delicious!* I was hooked.

One evening in a very elegant Boston restaurant, Hoby decided to teach me about fine desserts. He ordered a dish for me that I had never tasted, a bitter chocolate mousse. Hoby went on and on about how fabulous it was going to be. I couldn't wait. With great expectations, I plunged my spoon into the mousse and brought a heaping portion to my mouth. I hated it.

Not wanting to hurt Hoby's feelings, I swallowed the mousse and, not so accidentally, dropped my spoon. There was no way I was going to eat another bite.

Hoby, ever the gentleman, ran to find a waiter, in search of a clean spoon. While he was away, I opened my napkin, dumped the mousse into it, and stuffed the napkin into my handbag. I then took Hoby's spoon and placed it in the empty dish. Hoby returned, clean spoon in hand, and was shocked to find that I had inhaled all of my mousse. I smiled sheepishly to give the impression that I was embarrassed. He was thrilled to think that I loved his dessert of choice. My plan had worked perfectly.

Upon leaving, I grabbed my handbag and clutched it ever so tightly under my arm, forgetting its contents. Hoby stepped in front of me to open the door. I turned to the maître d' to say good-bye and noticed a trail of mousse droppings all the way to the door. Thank God Hoby never knew (until now—sorry, Hoby).

Hoby arranged for me to have my very own charge account at Trader Vic's. Though it was quite a treat for a poor girl like me not to have to look at prices when I ordered food, I never abused the privilege.

With every passing day I could feel that there was something more than just music in the fresh air of the sixties, and I was breathing deep, taking it all in. It was the beginning of a great liberation. Fortunately for me, I knew how to have a good time while keeping my feet planted firmly on the ground. I'm not going to pretend that I didn't try a few things, or claim that I never inhaled, but truly, I didn't drink and, except for the very occasional glass of wine or champagne, still don't. No earthly stimulation has ever gotten me as high as singing has.

One day, as part of Hoby's Eliza Doolittle Grooming Program, he said we should go to hear this girl sing at the Psychedelic Supermarket, which is how and where I first saw and heard Janis Joplin and her band, Big Brother and the Holding Company.

I remember that night so vividly. There she was, standing on the stage with a jug of moonshine she kept drinking from while she sang. Janis had this raspy, loud, belting voice that seemed to me so startlingly out of place with the rest of her stage presentation. She sported wild, unkempt hair and wore a long hippie dress with no bra. I had never seen anything like it before in my life! I couldn't believe that any woman, not to mention someone with a large bosom, would dare to get up on the stage without undergarments! My parents had taught me to *always* wear slips and girdles in public to make sure nothing ever moved around. "Don't give boys any reason to concentrate on the body—keep the focus on the brain" was my mother's mantra, and here was this Janis chick sloshing around half naked!

Quite honestly, I was so distracted by her appearance I almost didn't hear her singing. I wanted to get up and leave. But once I settled down and moved beyond my own preconceived notions, I began to appreciate what an amazing singer she was. Her voice and her phrasing sent chills down my spine. Hoby wanted me to study Janis's vocal freedom and her naturally relaxed stage presence. Looking back, I realize how fortunate I was to have seen Janis Joplin live.

✳

One Sunday in the spring of 1966, I found myself doing one of the things I loved most, walking alone and deep in thought along the Boston Common. The sky was just beginning to turn dark, an east wind was kicking up, and, just as I had that time when I was a little girl, I got caught up in the rustling of the leaves. I stood there watching the trees swaying all around me and once again felt the presence of God. It was my belief in Him that I was going to draw upon, as events no one could foresee were about to unfold.

I hadn't been doing well in high school. Singing with the

band and hanging out with Hoby had left me little time for studying, and as a result my grades had slipped. I knew I could do better, but high school seemed so boring in contrast to the excitement of singing in a rock 'n' roll band. Nothing could compare with that! I wanted to drop out of school and get myself a part-time day job. I poured over the newspapers until one day I found an ad for a job that looked appealing. I decided to skip school and head downtown with two of my friends, both of whom also wanted to find jobs.

We were walking along when ahead of us an old woman turned onto the street we were on, headed in the same direction. Almost simultaneously, three teenage boys ran past us toward the old woman. I caught a glimpse of one of the boys and immediately recognized him from church. His mother was a friend of our family. Without thinking, as he flew by, I said, "Hey, how are you doing? Why aren't you in school?"

"Why aren't you?" he yelled back

Before I knew what was happening, one of the boys punched the old woman right in the face. I was shocked! I screamed to my friend, "Don't run, don't run!"

The woman fell back and her head hit the sidewalk with a loud thump. One of the boys then grabbed her handbag, and they all took off running.

I ran over to the old woman, knelt down, and saw a deep gash on her chin where she'd been hit. I asked her if she was all right. Only then did I realize she was unconscious. I found out later she was deaf, which was why she hadn't heard the boys coming. Her eyes were open wide and frozen.

I put my hand on her stomach to see if she was breathing. She wasn't. I knew I had to give her artificial respiration, which scared me. I had no choice. So I took a deep breath, leaned over, and just as I was about to breathe into her mouth, I felt a gust of air coming from her as she suddenly began breathing again. Her facial wound began dripping blood. I held her until an ambulance appeared. The paramedics swarmed over us, and in all the confusion I grabbed my friends' hands and we took off.

I was cutting school, and I knew that if I hung around, I was sure to get in trouble with my parents, my father especially. I didn't need any of that, not now.

The old woman was in a coma for a week before she died. I read in the newspapers how the charges against the three boys, still at large, would change from attempted robbery to manslaughter, or possibly murder. A chill went down my spine. I knew I could identify at least one of the boys. I didn't know what to do. I was terrified. I prayed that the police would never find me, and that somehow I could avoid getting involved.

My secret began weighing heavily on my conscience. One day I heard on the local news that the police were actively looking for witnesses. My heart almost stopped. That meant me! If they found me, I'd have to tell the truth and betray a friend. Finally, I went to my aunt Mary and confided in her, trusting her sound advice. "Somebody has to stop those boys before they hurt someone else," she said, adding, "If they had robbed your grandmother, what would you do?" She was absolutely right, and I knew it. I immediately called the police department and told them that I had witnessed the attack on the old woman.

The officer suggested coming over to our house, and I told him that was out of the question. Instead, I asked him to meet me around the corner. He said he'd be there in fifteen minutes.

He showed up as planned. I told him the name of the boy and what I'd seen, and he left. Over the next several weeks all three boys were arrested, and, sure enough, I was called to testify against them at the trial. Their lawyer emphasized the one thing I wanted to keep a secret, that I had skipped school that day. He made it sound as if I were a cheap whore, walking the streets in broad daylight just looking for trouble. It was a terrible experience for me, made even worse by my family attending the trial and sitting next to all the families of the boys. I was under official protection, as the police feared possible retaliation.

It turns out that this group of boys had been terrorizing the neighborhood, for more than two whole years, harassing old people and stealing handbags from old ladies to the tune of thousands of dollars.

Even after the guilty verdicts were handed down, I knew I wasn't out of the woods. These boys had friends, dangerous friends, and we feared it was only a matter of time before one or more came after me. I began receiving threats.

Except for the time I was involved with the trial, I managed to keep most of my performance dates with the Crow. We played many nearby colleges and most of the clubs in Boston. In an unforeseen moment of good timing, the Crow received an offer to play in New York.

✳

I was nineteen and it was about a month before the Crow was supposed to debut in New York at the Purple Onion. While crossing off days on my calendar in anticipation of my trip, I realized I had missed my menstrual cycle. Surely I hadn't been that promiscuous, had I? My manager at that time, Bernie, told me he knew someone who could make my period come. I was so relieved.

The next Thursday afternoon, I was taken to the house of a woman who had been a nurse. I wa terrified. She injected me with some liquid concoction—I have no idea what it was, but it was supposed to start my period again. After a half hour of waiting, nothing happened. I went home.

That evening I began to have some minor discomfort. By the next morning I was in excruciating pain. My body temperature shot up, and I felt like I was on fire. I managed to call my cousin, who was the only one at home, for help. Then without warning, I felt something break inside me, and I started to bleed. I passed out in the stairwell. My cousin quickly managed to get me into a taxi and rushed me to the Boston City Hospital, the same place I was born. In and out of consciousness, I kept crying, "Don't tell my parents. Don't tell my parents." But she did. My mother raced over to the hospital.

The doctors didn't think I was going to make it. However, after two days of extreme fever, my temperature began to subside. The doctors operated and turned the situation around. It took years for my reproductive organs, intestines, and nervous system to recover. And to think it was all self-induced.

I felt I was paying a price for my disobedience to my parents and, more importantly, to God. A strange darkness set in. I felt exiled to this body of imperfections, ashamed, so unredeemable, and deeply, deeply lost.

Under any other circumstances, my parents would have absolutely forbidden me to go to New York, but because of the threats I had received, they had no objections. They were thankful for the opportunity to put some distance between me and the potential dangers in Boston. My father knew it was better to have me alive in New York than dead in Boston.

The fabled Greenwich Village, like the Boston scene, was bursting with new venues. Thanks to acts like Richie Havens and the monumental arrival of Bob Dylan, the Village had surpassed Beantown as the East Coast mecca of folk-rock.

On the night we played the Purple Onion, a scout from RCA Records caught our act, came backstage, and offered the band a recording contract.

Or, to be more accurate, he offered me a contract. The scout had heard something in my voice he liked, but he had little interest in the Crow. It was an awkward situation. He was willing to sign the Crow to a separate deal if the band wanted. However, the band was headed for a breakup. Like so many bands, the Crow had developed internal disputes over direction and rivalries over leadership. The news that I would leave only made matters worse.

I talked the situation over with Hoby. He agreed it was the right thing to do and said that he would try to keep the band together long enough to help out on a demo, but we both knew the band was about to be history. As for our relationship, that too was on a rocky road, although I still wanted Hoby to be a part of my life. After all, he was my best friend.

In the midst of all the drama, I almost lost track of the most important thing: RCA had just offered me a recording contract!

3

Touched by an Angel

It was the summer of '68. I was living in Greenwich Village and loving every bit of it—the streets, the coffee shops, the people, the pervasive heat, and, most of all, the *beat* and the *spirit* permeating the Village. I was staying in an apartment above the Café Wha? on MacDougal Street that I shared with a French girl who was going out with the manager of the Crow. She was supposed to keep an eye on me, but she was hardly ever around, which was fine with me. I loved being alone.

Our apartment was on the top floor of a four-story walk-up, a typical hippie pad complete with pillows on the floor, a big fluffy futon, black lights, incense, candles, lots of green plants with the obligatory macramé, and the signature New York City unwashed windows, but at least the windows weren't nailed shut. I used to make myself a cup of herbal tea, open the window, crawl out on the ledge with my feet dangling down, and people-watch. No matter how late or how early it was, the

Performing with the Crow, circa 1968. *Photographer unknown*

crowds always made it look like four in the afternoon. I had a game I used to play. I'd sort the passersby in my head, separating the tourists who'd come downtown to gape at the real-live hippies and buy souvenir T-shirts from the neighborhood regulars who walked by every day. From the safety of my perch, the people passing by became my secret means of daily entertainment. I'd make up stories about the interesting faces as they went by and try to imagine all the details of their lives: who they were, where they were coming from, where they were going, what they did with their lives. It was a great lesson in writing. Summer in the city by myself introduced me to a whole new vista for my creative imagination.

My favorite thing was to sleep late into the afternoon. It was the best part of being a singer, one of the side benefits of what people call "musicians' hours." Coming, as I had, from such a constantly crowded and busy household, it was a treat for me to wake up to relative silence. Sometimes I'd feel a momentary rush of loneliness. I was, after all, living without my family for the first time in my life, and that was difficult. However, I knew that I had landed at the door of a wonderfully musical world, which was another kind of reality, and that I had undoubtedly arrived at the heart of a new generation.

I liked to take barefoot walks over to the center of Washington Square Park, one of the most beautiful places I've ever seen, not so much physically but rather communally. There was always a great influx of young and talented people who had gravitated there from all walks of New York City life. It was *the* place to hear musicians playing and singing, where everybody could stand side by side and be completely equal. When someone was playing for the crowd, there were no races, no gangs, and no rivalries, just a lot of cool people enjoying the music.

I got to know a lot of the park musicians, and I still think they were among the best I've ever heard. Some sang in groups and did beautiful, intricate, five-part New York–style doo-wop harmonies; some played fabulous folk-style finger-picking guitar; and some sang their own new and exciting songs. Admirers would throw money in their hats, providing food for the day.

Having arrived early that summer, I was about to experience an adult dose of what the Lovin' Spoonful had called "Hot town, summer in the city." There was a consistent smell that radiated off the cement sidewalks, redolent of the Village's mix of patchouli, sweat, sex, and youth. I loved to wade through the thick pool of heady, unwashed youth. On one particularly hot day, a young black man grabbed my arm as I was coming out of the park, yanked me around, and said, "Sister, you don't walk around with no shoes! You're too beautiful for that! You go home right now and put some sandals on! Don't you know black is beautiful?"

I was terrified! I ran right back to my place and put my sandals on and never left the apartment barefoot again. After that I'd see him in the street all the time, and eventually we became friends. I wondered who he really was, if he hadn't been put there to watch out for me. You never know!

✳

We finished cutting a few demos for RCA Records in early August 1968. After the last recording session a friend of mine picked me up and, to celebrate, offered to take me anywhere I wanted to go. I knew he was waiting for me to choose some club or hot nightspot, but instead I said, "I want to go down to the Bowery." He said, "The Bowery? Are you serious?" I replied, "Yes, I really want to go to the Bowery."

Sure enough, as soon as we got down to the Bowery we promptly got lost. Now, the Bowery is not where you want to get lost. We were surrounded by abandoned low-income tenements and a multitude of disenfranchised people. We were walking down the street when out of the darkness an old man emerged, dragging his feet as he came toward us. He looked like an older version of Kenny Rogers, only in rags, and with a shock of white hair and a long, scraggly beard. I noticed an intense white light coming off his face. I had never seen anything like it before! I quickly turned to my friend and said, "Do you see what I see?" He nodded, a combination of wonder and disbelief.

The white-haired man kept coming toward me, until he was right in front of my face. Before I could do anything, he grabbed my hand. "Don't be afraid," he said in a soft, soothing voice, and instantly my entire *being* relaxed. "Listen to me, I want to tell you something. You're going to meet a man, take a test, pass the test, and you will have an opportunity to cross the waters. You must cross the waters! You have an incredible ability to write; you'll be more famous as a writer than what you're doing now.

"Don't be lazy," he added. "Now, do what I say!" He patted my hand, turned around, and walked back in the direction from which I'd come.

My friend and I looked at each other for a second or two, and when we turned back to look at the stranger ... *he had disappeared!*

It was weird, really weird. It was as if for a split second we had crossed over into another dimension. Time itself had seemed to stand still. When we finally realized what had happened, my friend and I both ran down the street looking for the man, but there wasn't a trace of him anywhere. It seemed as though once again Providence had extended its divine hand into my reality. At that moment I knew I had been touched by an angel.

The whole thing struck me as spooky and yet amazing. I started to weep right there in the street—not tears of sadness or fear, but an outpouring of all my emotions that had been stirred by the angel's vision and prophetic words.

I went back to my place to lie down for a while, to try to make sense out of what had just happened. I fell asleep for a few hours, woke up feeling a little more settled, and started vocalizing, my favorite way of relaxing. After a few minutes there was a knock on the door. I opened it and saw my roommate, Genevieve, standing with the Broadway producer Bertrand Castelli, the director of the upcoming German production of the new musical *Hair,* which was taking the theatrical world by storm.

Theater itself was undergoing rapid change in New York. Productions of such radical shows as *MacBird, Fortune and Men's Eyes,* and *Hair* were upstaging the more conventional productions. *Hair* had begun life in a club called Cheetah before being reconceived as an off-Broadway musical by Joseph Papp's downtown theater organization.

Genevieve introduced me to Bertrand, who told me he had heard my singing as they were coming down the hallway. He said I had a great voice and asked if I would come down Thursday afternoon to audition for the European production of *Hair* that he was casting.

I showed up at the audition looking like the kind of hippie/street-cutie I figured they were looking for, all decked out in a short minidress with ancient Rome–style sandals that laced up to my knees. After what I thought was a pretty good audition, Bertrand asked, "Can you travel?"

I replied, "How far can I go?"

"England, France, or Germany—take your pick," he said.

I yelled, "I'll take Germany," remembering that Daddy had spoken German around the house when I was a child. Bertrand then told me that I had the part and they would contact me in the next two weeks and take care of all the arrangements.

I was happily walking on air down the streets of midtown Manhattan, my mind a million miles away. Suddenly two young, well-dressed black men who looked like they had just stepped out of a business meeting approached me. One of them asked me a question, and when I turned to him, the other one went around to my other side and he, too, started asking me questions. They both spoke so fast it sounded like double-talk to me. I couldn't make out a word of what they were saying. Then it dawned on me I was being scammed! They must have seen the recognition in my eyes, because one of the men grabbed me

47

tightly by my arm and said, very loudly, "No, you're going home to your kids! Just look how you're dressed! Where do you think you're going?"

What? I had no idea what he was talking about! From the corner of my eye I could see a police officer standing on a nearby corner. I started yelling at them to let me go. "Stop, I'm not your wife!" I screamed.

One of the men screamed back: "I SAID YOU CAN'T COME HERE ON THE STREET DRESSED LIKE THAT. YOU'RE GOING HOME TO YOUR KIDS RIGHT NOW!"

By now I was sure the cop had seen what was happening to me. But he didn't move or say a word. I was really terrified, knowing I was in some very big trouble if the police wouldn't help me.

Each of the men now had me by one of my arms, and they literally lifted me off the ground and carried me that way for blocks, right in the middle of the Garment District, as if I were a piece of merchandise!

When we got to one corner I saw an empty cab, and figured it was my only chance. I took a deep breath, lifted my arms straight up in the air, bent my elbows, and hit both of them in their ribs as hard as I could. That bought me a few seconds, during which I managed to break away, grab the cab's door handle, open it, and dive for the backseat with everything I had. At that moment, the light changed and the driver pulled away. He turned to look at me and suddenly realized I was in trouble. I was lying flat across the seat with my feet still out the door and couldn't catch my breath enough to speak. I waved for him to go, as I knew the two men would be on me in a second. I prayed the driver wouldn't hand me over to those thugs.

He must have seen the fear in my face, because he turned back to the wheel and took off. "Are you okay, miss?" he asked. But I still could not speak. Finally I uttered my home address.

He took me downtown to my home in the Village, where I felt safe. I locked myself in the apartment and tried to pull myself together. My accosters could very well have been just a couple of local muggers, but the only explanation that made any sense was that they were somehow connected to the criminals in Boston. At that time, I felt those two men were part of an elaborate kidnapping scheme to make me pay for giving the police the name of that boy. I knew that from now on I was going to have to be more careful. Suddenly, even New York City was no longer far enough away from Boston to make me feel safe.

Two days later I got a call from Bertrand Castelli's office confirming the offer for a featured role in the German cast of *Hair,* to be produced in Munich that September. I had to get far, far away. All I needed was a passport, because there was a plane ticket already waiting for me.

Two seconds later I called back and accepted the offer without telling my parents.

✳

Many times in the ensuing years I've thought about that man in the Bowery. Who was he? How did he know what he knew? As extraordinary as it may seem to some, I've come to believe it must have been the hand of God coming to me through an angel, sent to redirect me toward my purpose, to guide me and to make sure I stayed on the path that He had chosen for me. Had he not appeared and described so accurately what was about to happen to me—the offer, the test, the journey over the waters—it is very likely I would not have been able to muster up the courage to go to Europe all by myself. I would have made a record or two with RCA and probably would have married Hoby, but as the incident at the Bowery clearly showed me, that was not my destiny. Nor was being kidnapped!

I knew that I had to go to Munich. Even if my father said no, I couldn't stay. I had made up my mind. I'd swim all the way to Europe if that's what it took, because nothing, nothing, was going to prevent me from fulfilling my destiny.

I decided to return to Boston to gather my things and make my good-byes. My parents were happy and relieved that I had returned home, believing that I was back for good. Before I told them what my plan actually was, I got all my papers together and finalized my travel arrangements. Only then did I have the courage to break the news to them. I first spoke to my mother, telling her that she had to talk to Daddy and convince him to let me go.

My father's initial reaction was "You're *what*? *You're doing what*? You met a man and he gave you money? He bought you a plane ticket and he's taking you to Germany? I don't think so, young lady! You're not going anywhere. You're going to your room."

When he finally began to calm down and I was able to talk to him, I told him I was still afraid that something was going to happen to me because of those boys I'd helped put in jail. I told him that the man who wanted me to go to Germany was a well-known and highly respected figure in the New York theater world. Daddy gradually began to come around, even if he remained a bit suspicious. He said, "*Well, I want to know who this man is. I want to talk to him myself!*"

That sounded reasonable to me. I called Bertrand that night and arranged for him to call my father the next day. He did, and they talked for a long time. My father listened to everything he had to say, hung up, thought about it for a long time, considered every aspect of the offer very carefully, and then made his decision. He was going to let me go!

A little later, Hoby called and asked if he could take me out for dinner. Things had cooled off between us ever since the record company had rejected the band. I hadn't seen him for a few months and figured he wanted to say good-bye and wish me well. I guess that's why I was totally unprepared for what happened after dinner when he pulled over on Parker Hill Avenue, turned to me, and said, "Will you marry me, Donna?"

"What!" I said. I was speechless.

Before I had a chance to say anything, he went on to tell me he had bought a town house in the Back Bay area of Boston for us. He told me he would wait for me for six months, the length of my German contract for *Hair,* and that when I returned to the States we would get married and move into the new house.

He was so sweet that night, and, yes, the offer was tempting, one that I would have died for not so very long ago. However, everything in my life had changed, including my feelings for Hoby. As hard as it was to admit, to myself as well as to him, I knew that whatever had been between us was finished, and that he wasn't to be my husband. I knew he had been a big and important part of my life. He'd been responsible for bringing me into the music business. He had given me the benefit of all his musical knowledge and cultural upbringing. For all that and more, I knew I would always have a special feeling in my heart for Hoby Cook.

I believed he had been brought into my life for a specific purpose, but it wasn't to turn me into a Boston housewife. Besides, I was the wrong color and from the wrong side of the tracks, and that would never change.

Our parting was bittersweet but inevitable, and even as we slipped into the melancholy of the past, I couldn't contain my excitement at moving forward into my future. For me, Hoby, the Crow, Boston, and the Village were already part of my past. I flew back to New York City to spend one last day there before boarding a plane for Germany. I phoned my daddy and he admitted that my going there was probably the best thing I could do, both for my career and for my safety. He knew it was a big chance for me, and if that gang was still looking for me, I'd probably be safer in Munich than in Harvard Square or New York. We said our final good-byes, and just before I hung up I heard my father say, "Good luck, Donna, and please be careful, because I won't be there to protect you."

I promised him I would, and with tears in my eyes I said,

"Daddy, remember, my dream is for you." I put the phone back on its cradle. That was it, I told myself. There was no turning back. My tomorrow was ahead.

On August 28, 1968, I stepped on a plane bound for Germany. *Hair* I come!

4

Life on the Autobahn

I was euphoric and a little bit scared. I was nineteen years old and flying alone halfway around the world to join the company of the musical *Hair*. The flight took nearly eight hours, and it was early morning when the plane finally landed in Munich. I had been told that I would be met by the music director, but there was no one to meet me. With no idea what accommodations had been arranged, I decided to head straight for the theater. I got to the taxi stand before someone tapped me on the shoulder. "Hi, I'm Steve," he said, "and this is Helga, my wife." It was the music director. Upon leaving the airport, I saw people dressed in traditional German clothing and noticed how clean everything was. I could feel the excitement that comes from the anticipation of the unknown.

I remember walking up the stairs of an old building and peeking into a room full of strange but interesting people. They were all standing in a circle around a black man who

Onstage with the German cast of *Hair*, circa 1968. I'm the one on the right. *Photographer unknown; photo courtesy of the Sudano family archives*

spoke a language I didn't understand. Nevertheless, from the smiles on everyone's faces, I felt completely welcome. They were in the middle of rehearsing and waved at me to come and join them. "Rehearsal," I thought to myself. "I'm exhausted."

During a break in the rehearsal I introduced myself to one of the actors, who told me his name was Ronnie. When he found out I had nowhere to stay, he offered to let me room with him temporarily. Ronnie was an American who had lived in Germany ever since being stationed there while serving in the U.S. military. When his tour of duty ended, he'd elected to stay in Munich. He was a very talented young actor and had managed to work in the Vienna Theater, which had led him to the role of Hud in this production of *Hair*.

I found Ronnie a bit cocky, and I suppose he had a right to be, having already made somewhat of a name and reputation for himself. Since being in Germany he'd worked steadily in movies, on TV, and in commercials. The key to his success was a simple combination: he was very handsome and talented, and, perhaps even more important, he was black. As I quickly came to understand, liberal postwar-generation Germans living in Munich wanted to make some sort of personal statement about the Civil Rights movement in America. Frequently that statement took the form of friendship, support, and work for anyone of color who happened to be from the States. Yippee! I was in the right place at the right time.

Ordinarily I would never have taken Ronnie or anyone else up on such living arrangements, but I was experiencing a rush of freedom the likes of which I had never felt before. My instincts told me I could trust him.

Apparently, I wasn't the only one without accommodations. All the Americans were in the same boat—no rooms, no cash, and no ability yet to understand German. As those first few hours passed, I began to appreciate Ronnie's invitation more and more, realizing how lucky I would be to have a seasoned guide for a roommate. Besides, he was a brother, and I felt comfortable.

Another major plus was that he spoke German *and* English, and seeing how, at the time, I didn't speak more than a few words of German, I figured Ronnie would be a great help in getting me through the first few intimidating weeks.

That day, I also met two girls in the company who I instantly liked. One of them was a blond German girl by the name of Christina who was fluent in English. To this day we remain very good friends; she is my soul sister. The other, Anna, was a beautiful girl who looked like the model Iman. All three of us were new to Munich as well as to acting as a profession. That made our bond of friendship that much tighter.

New friends, new country, new show, new *everything*. My life was undergoing an especially radical metamorphosis, and the change was more acute for me than for Ronnie, Christina, or Anna, because I was coming from a strict, church-influenced, traditional New England upbringing. The more I thought about it, the more I realized that it was true: God gives you the family you're born with, the ones who help you become the person you're supposed to grow up to be, but it is your friends who

I am in the center performing "White Boys" in the German production of *Hair*. *Photo by Dagmar*

become your family of choice. So upon my arrival in Germany, I tried to choose my family carefully.

The first time I went with Ronnie to his place, I was shocked at how small the apartment actually was. It was hardly bigger than a college dorm room, with one small sink for a kitchen, an outside bathroom, and one twin bed. The room was no larger than a huge closet. Once I put my bags down I had to climb over them just to get to the bed, while Ronnie slept on the floor (or what was left of it). Still, I was grateful to have a place to stay, and I was determined to make the most of Ronnie's generous offer. Hey, let's face it: it was free and that was a good thing.

We lasted all of two weeks before we realized our living arrangements weren't going to work, at least not in this confined place. I suggested that it might be a good idea for us to try to find a bigger place. We hardly had any money, so we got together with several of the other cast members, including Anna, and found a mostly vacant building with maisonette apartments, complete with cute little balconies. The rooms were small and quaint, but compared to what Ronnie and I had been living in, I thought they looked as luxurious as the castles on the Rhine!

The company always started rehearsals late in the morning (I liked that!) by doing touchy-feely warm-up exercises. Like everything else, this was something I had never experienced before, which is not to say I didn't like it. One interesting side effect was that we all became very close very quickly. A few of us in the company were still under twenty years old, and our youth certainly contributed to the newly inspired freedom we were all experiencing. It didn't take long for people to start pairing off.

The interesting thing for me about doing *Hair* was how the troupe itself became one constantly evolving family. Our lives mirrored the lives of the characters. The company was really about two things: the staged presentation of a lifestyle dramatized by us in *Hair* and the actual lifestyle being lived by us offstage. Every night we'd go to clubs together, after which we'd all visit the homes of friends, and while we were there someone would inevitably take out a guitar. There would be hours of singing and laughing and, of course, loving. If there was a European Woodstock, this was it!

Our production was a huge hit, and the leads, of which I was one, became instant local celebrities. I sang several key songs in the show—in German, of course, which I quickly learned—including "Aquarius," "White Boys," and, along with the others, "Let the Sunshine In." I had solo parts in "Good Morning Starshine," and "Three-Five-Zero-Zero." I also appeared in the controversial naked scene at least once.

Everyone in the cast was required to appear in the naked scene, although after my first performance the police showed up and told the producers that any performer under the age of twenty-one could not continue to appear nude. After that, the three of us minors became the "shakers" who held the slitted white sheet in front of the others, to give the effect of clouds from which the actors "emerged." Let me say, there was nothing lewd or lascivious about any of the nudity. The lights were set in such a way that no one was really all that exposed, and it

HAARE

(HAIR)

THEATER IN DER BRIENNERSTRASSE

I am on the left in a promotional poster for the German production of *Hair*, circa 1968. *Photo by Dagmar*

was more a celebration of the freedom of nature, with absolutely no pornographic suggestion.

We were photographed everywhere we went, and our pictures were always in the newspapers. We were often interviewed on radio and television. We'd wear the wildest clothing,
like granny boots, gladiator sandals, bell-bottom pants, and the
ever-popular Afro and long hairstyles. We were sent out in the
early afternoon to nearby towns to promote the show, trying to
build an audience with people who would not normally travel
into the city to see us. Everywhere we went we were greeted by
huge crowds. We'd do a number from the show in the town
square and leave as the new local heroes, our pockets filled with
receipts for sold tickets. It was my first taste of true celebrity,
and I loved it!!

Ronnie and I had by now become one of the dating couples
of the company. He had appointed himself as ruler over my life.
Away from the show, he was all business, which somehow surprised me. He was into promoting himself and his career, with
everything and everyone else having to line up behind. Once in
a while he would throw me a bone and I would sing with him
on a jingle or on a movie soundtrack. That part was fun, and I
was grateful, but it bothered me how controlling Ronnie could
be. The message was very clear: I was not to invade his professional turf. If someone asked who I was and whether I was
available, Ronnie would cut me off and say I couldn't speak the
language. But I was quickly learning.

Before too long I began to get personally noticed for my
work in *Hair*. A few weeks after the show opened, I was singled

out by one critic both for my voice and for my acting. I had a natural stage presence, a combination of approachability and American black street moves. To say the least, my appearance made me stick out in a Munich crowd! Bobbing my head to Jimi Hendrix, I was already quite tall, but I stood even taller in the platform shoes I liked to wear, topped off with a towering Angela Davis–style Afro. If anyone was going to get noticed, it was going to be me. There weren't that many black women in Germany at that time, and German men marveled at us. I could barely walk down the street without being followed by photographers wanting to snap their first picture of a black woman in an Afro.

These were the years of the Civil Rights movement, and I was well aware of the antagonism that had emerged back in the States, especially toward the more militant representatives of Black Power. Angela Davis was one of my personal heroes. While she was also generally reviled in America, I thought she was among the most beautiful and eloquent spokespersons of her time. In Germany, Angela Davis was regarded as a courageous young folk hero. Many young black women living in Germany took on the look of the big Afro as their statement of freedom, black beauty, and personal empowerment in the new emerging pop culture. The statement said, "I see my blackness as beautiful. I don't need anyone's approval."

Not surprisingly, I got offered a lot of modeling work. Surprisingly, I didn't see myself as model material, as I was just an ordinary girl . . . a plain Jane. I probably wouldn't have done any modeling at all, except that I had become very good friends

My boyfriend Ronnie and I in the German production of *Hair*.
Photo by Dagmar

with Will McBride. At that time Will was one of the top fashion photographers and worked for one of the biggest German fashion magazines. I loved his work, and he took me under his wing. When he approached me about posing, I was hesitant. But the more I saw of his work, the more fascinated I became. Will liked to capture his subjects on film from where they lived inside their head. He used distortion techniques a lot, which really appealed to me. For example, if you fiddled with your hands a lot, he would shoot them in the foreground and make them enormous in the finished photo.

I got to know Will and his family quite well, and through him I gained entrée into the highly cerebral German clique of artists and intellectuals.

For the first time in my life I felt like an equal, and I thought that maybe I could fit in with this artistic group. I wanted to learn how to paint better. I had taken a couple of art classes my last year in high school, but that was nothing compared to the opportunity I now had to extend my creative horizons among some of the most talented artists in Europe, without fear of being laughed at or dismissed.

It was all part of my fairy-tale existence in a beautiful country that I had completely fallen in love with. The Germans had completely rebuilt their country since the end of World War II, and along with this physical rebirth had arisen the desire of a new generation to live well and be free. Indeed, Germany represented a movement of personal liberation for me as well, and I was living in an artistic and cultural bohemia, a creative heaven.

The simplest things, like ordering food, became a significant new part of my life. Ham and eggs were now *Spiegeleier mit Schinken.* My first taste of *Leberknödelsuppe,* liver-dumpling soup, was a revelation! As a kid I'd grown up hating even the *idea* of liver. It reminded me of the sole of a shoe. I had only eaten liver a few times in my life, and even then with great reluctance, so I was totally unprepared for how fabulous I found *Leberknödelsuppe* to be. I made it a point to eat as many new foods as I could and to educate myself in all these unusual tastes I'd never had before. Not only was I ready for this change, I *craved* it. Every new food, every new form of architecture, every new expression, every antique I discovered was a door to a whole *new* world. I'd always had a fondness for history, and now I was walking through the living embodiment of everything I had ever studied. I was rapidly absorbing a "hands-on" education I could never have gotten any other way. This was the way I needed to learn.

Being in Germany made me realize just how young America really was. In Germany I was stepping into centuries of European history, fixed in stone, the product of civilizations that had come and gone long before America had even been discovered.

Imagine falling asleep in a quaint little German bed-and-breakfast to awaken with the dawn to the smell of *lebkuchen* (gingerbread) and Ronnie calling me from outside in a horse-drawn carriage. I quickly ran to the balcony, threw open the doors, and stepped barefoot into two feet of white, virgin snow. It was a real-life Christmas snow globe, with Neuschwanstein

Me looking like Angela Davis. *Photographer unknown; photo courtesy of Carl-Walter Holthoff*

castle towering above us. (Neuschwanstein was Walt Disney's inspiration for Cinderella's castle.) It was a mystical and surreal vision I will never forget, one every girl should be allowed to experience at least once.

They say comedy is one of the hardest styles of acting to perfect. Imagine trying to perform comedy in both another language and another culture. There are numerous innuendos that must be learned so you can begin to understand what makes something funny. Learning to communicate onstage in a foreign language was probably one of the best acting lessons in the world, because it forced me to act with my whole body rather than using just my words. The fact that I succeeded on even a basic performance level in *Hair* is an accomplishment I remain very proud of.

However, my greatest achievement during this period came with learning how to be a whole and independent human being. Looking back, I'm amazed that I packed up and moved to another country. It's a good thing there wasn't much time to think about it, because had I had that luxury, I'm positive I would never have made such a radical decision to take a journey that would wind up changing my life in every possible way.

✳

When my initial six-month contract with the company was up, I decided to remain in Germany and re-sign for another year and a half. I also agreed to travel all over the Continent with the show, which opened another whole new world for me. While doing *Hair* in Vienna, the entire cast got to hang out with

Leonard Bernstein. If you're familiar with *Hair,* you know that at the end of every show the cast always invited the audience members up onstage to dance. It's part of the original script. Leonard was so taken by our passion that he came right up and boogied with us! His spontaneous participation made headlines around the world. When the curtain came down, he invited the whole cast to his apartment in Vienna.

We got to know Lenny very well. (All his friends called him Lenny; it was never Leonard.) It was a great experience.

Life illuminates our dreams in so many ways. This is a lesson I learned more clearly in Europe than I had anywhere else or at any other time in my life. Remember that photo of a young Bill Clinton shaking hands with President Kennedy? I had a similar experience, though with no historical significance. One night, quite unexpectedly, I met one of my great heroes, the spectacular, legendary Josephine Baker. We were both performing at the Deutsches Museum in Munich in 1972. She was the headliner, and I was one of the singers in the opening act. I watched her from the wings, and when she was through with her show, she saw me as she was walking off the stage. She put her hand out and said, "Please help me down." She was wearing a skintight bodysuit with sparkles all over it and a big plumed hat—I was completely swept away as I helped her all the way to her dressing room.

Josephine Baker is the only person I've ever asked for an autograph. There were so many parallels between her life and mine. She'd moved to Europe as a young girl, and had lived and gained fame there, and so had I. She was a black American singer who loved performing overseas, and so was I. It has always stayed in my heart and my soul that I was the one whom she chose to help her come off the stage, just as my own career was on the rise. It was as though she were passing the baton to me.

Many years later, the people who owned the rights to her life story thought I was the only person who should play her on-screen. They had asked Princess Grace of Monaco, a great friend of Josephine's, whom she saw in the role of the great lady. The princess said without hesitation that it had to be Donna Summer. I never did get to make that movie, but to this day when young people tell me how much they love my music and how important it has been to them in their lives, I am reminded of my own appreciation of Josephine Baker. I feel blessed to have been able to make a positive impact, and who knows, a young fan might grow up to be a legend and remember the time when, for the briefest of moments, the paths of our destinies crossed.

With my growing European success came a new kind of responsibility. I began to feel an obligation to be "on" twenty-four hours a day. I was to be available for any and all press at any time, as if I were an ambassador for whatever show I was in, for blacks living in Germany, and for Americans abroad. Everywhere I went, people would come right up to me as if they knew me, as if I were a part of their family. It was all well and good, until very slowly, more and more of my life began to belong less and less to me. Somewhere along the way the scales tipped in the wrong direction, signaling the beginning of what was to be some very rough pavement on the road of my life on the autobahn.

5

Love in Vienna

While living in Germany I became acquainted with the local blue bloods, a class of society that simply doesn't exist in America. The closest thing we have to it in America are super-rich older families like the Rockefellers and the Vanderbilts. The *Adlich,* as they are called, are the dethroned royalty of Europe, who have no actual political power but plenty of social status and (most of the time) enough money to keep so-called ordinary people interested in every aspect of their lives. Occasionally, perhaps as a form of social recreation, the blue bloods allow an entertainer into their crazy world of castles and privilege. They regard these chosen entertainers as their personal court jesters, and in their way of thinking, just being allowed into their presence is payment enough.

Because of the fame I garnered through *Hair,* I was one of those given entrée into that world. The one thing that was required of me while among the *Adlich* was to look young, cute, and

On a peaceful hilltop just outside Vienna, my friend Ulf snapped this picture, which is one of my favorites. *Photo by Ulf Baumhauckl*

fashionable and show up at whatever fabulous functions to which I was invited. If a piano or a guitar happened to be present, and one always seemed to be, I was expected to perform a number from the show to an unrehearsed but somehow always perfect accompaniment. The trick was to be available at the drop of a hat, for a night of fun in the great restaurants, villas, and clubs of Europe.

I also used to enjoy visiting U.S. Army clubs, like the Tilberry and the Blue Bird, where everybody blended into one giant cultural potpourri—American soldiers, European society types, working-class people, and, of course, musicians, actors, singers, and dancers. Nobody ever went home early. Once you showed up for a night in these clubs, the party ended only when the sun came up and someone suggested a great place to go for breakfast. Then you'd hang for another couple of hours, listening to live jazz over coffee, Brötchen, sausage, and eggs. Finally, we'd all go home and sleep until the early afternoon, then do whatever job and/or promo we were supposed to do. We'd meet again in the café, then head back to the theater and get ready to do a show. Afterward, we'd go out and live the party all over again. For me, those days and nights seemed as if they'd never end. Life was big and delicious.

While I was performing in Vienna in *Hair*, I asked some cast members if they could recommend a good doctor I could see for an earache I couldn't shake. As it happened, the company of *Hair* had a doctor on permanent call, and he happened to be in the theater that afternoon. So I called for him.

In he walked, decked out in a green velvet jacket, with a fancy mustache and long brown hair. At first I didn't believe he was really a doctor. No doctor I'd ever seen before had ever looked as good as this one. After much reassurance that he was for real, I followed him cautiously into the backstage examination room.

It took only half a glance for me to realize that I was wildly attracted to this man. His name was Dr. Meyer (not actually, but I want to keep his real name private) and I remember telling myself, Uh-uuh, am I going to have my hands full.

I just knew I had to get to know him. There was an almost uncontrollable attraction between us, the kind I imagined happened only in movies, and I didn't know what to do. "I think you should come to my office tomorrow and let me take a better look at you," he said.

"Do you think you can help me?" I asked coyly.

He looked me right in the eyes, as if he were going to devour me. Panting, he caught himself and said, "I'm sure I've got something that will make you feel . . ."

I kept my appointment the next morning, and with it a series of secret rendezvous began, under the guise of receiving medical attention. I mean, he was a doctor and I was getting his attention right away. As we got to know each other, I began to realize just how amazing he really was and that it was time to examine my relationship with Ronnie. Dr. Meyer was a psychiatrist, an excellent photographer, a real nature lover, and an intellectual, in addition to being a medical doctor. Somehow, he was destined to be someone who would teach me how to live. Above all, Dr. Meyer taught me not to be afraid to put myself on the edge and experience life to the fullest.

The famous opera singer Julie McGuiness and I have a comedic photo
session in Vienna. I'm on the ground.

Photographer unknown; photo courtesy of the Gaines family

Several months after leaving the Viennese production of *Hair* I went back to Vienna to perform in *Porgy and Bess* and *Showboat.* One night Dr. Meyer took me to dine with his family at one of those beautiful Austrian castles in the countryside. It was a wonderful dinner, and by the time the evening was over, I knew I was head-over-heels crazy about Dr. Meyer. He was so irresistibly charming.

There was a major problem, however. Dr. Meyer was so successful I couldn't see him as often as I wanted, which was all the time. I now had the luxury of more free time, and more money. When not with Dr. Meyer, I spent every spare second exploring Vienna. My first impression of Vienna was that it was a European version of New York (or maybe New York was an American version of Vienna). It had the same sensibilities and, like New York, a tremendous connection to the arts. There was the opera, the famous balls, the ballet, the classical orchestras, and an endless number of fabulous restaurants, scattered through some of the greatest neighborhoods I'd ever explored. On top of everything else, Vienna had a terrific mix of people from all walks of life, and from every corner of the world.

The production companies of *Porgy and Bess* and *Showboat* that I performed with were superior, affording me the privilege of working with world-class singers. They were highly re-garded and highly paid. To be able to work with these profes-sionals, even though I had no formal background or training, was a further affirmation of my own abilities. Though it was a great experience, I realized after a while that I was singing opera with a rock 'n' roll heart.

While in Vienna, I began to suffer from what would turn into a case of chronic insomnia that often left me tired and moody. It got so bad I agreed to take the "sleeping cures" Dr. Meyer suggested. I was partying too much; I had to take a break. He said he knew a retreat in the Viennese countryside where they specialized in alternative treatments. He drove me there, and when we arrived, I was surprised to discover that the clinic was nothing but a primitive farmhouse with no electricity, no bathroom, *nothing*. It was all part of Dr. Meyer's secret plan. He felt I was working too hard, and maybe playing a little too hard as well, which was the cause of my insomnia. Now he insisted I take the kind of rest he knew I medically needed.

I stared in disbelief as Dr. Meyer rhapsodized about how great it would be for me to get up at six o'clock every day to collect fresh eggs from the chickens and get milk from the neighboring farm. I remember thinking to myself that the only time I was willing to be up at six o'clock in the morning was when I was already up from the night before. Did I really need *this* much of a cure? I guess I did, because I was too exhausted to resist.

Dr. Meyer and I and another couple who were there with us were all supposed to sleep on the same floor of the most rustic farmhouse I'd ever seen. I was tired but I couldn't settle down, and these friends of Dr. Meyer's offered me a cup of tea secretly spiked with schnapps. When I woke up the next morning, I felt so woozy from the alcohol. I would never have taken the "cure" had I known I would feel this way. I looked across the room and saw the other couple squeezed into a one-man sleeping bag. Suddenly I realized, to my horror, that Dr. Meyer and I were also *in one sleeping bag*! Even though I had strong feelings for Dr. Meyer, we had never been intimate. This was too much!

My eyes welled up. My pride was hurt, so hurt, and my heart was broken at having been taken advantage of by someone I had trusted so much. How could he? How could he? I was shocked. I jumped out of the sleeping bag and ran outside. He followed and tried to console me, but I just kept running. I said, "Don't touch me!"

"You don't understand," he said, trying to make me stop, but I couldn't help myself. "Please," he went on, running after me, "I've been waiting so long! *Forgive me!! I was wrong!!*"

I started crying and shouted, "Take me home!"

"Listen to me," he shouted. "Everyone else is still sleeping!"

"Then stop shouting!" I yelled at him. I began to walk away, and for the first time, in the early fog, I noticed a declining black sky and the thin strip of daylight that cut through it against the rust-colored earth. I felt suspended then, and all at once I had a realization about this mystical Austrian setting. I felt in a way that Dr. Meyer and I were Adam and Eve, that we were in Eden, and that we were the only two people in the world.

Just then he came up behind me and aggressively grabbed me and pulled me toward him. Through the mist of the dawn, I could see the thunder in his eyes and he could feel the lightning in mine. In that moment, I knew him completely.

I wasn't going anywhere.

My early days in Germany. I'm about twenty-one years old and standing on a stage in Hamburg. *Photographer unknown; photo courtesy of the Summer archives*

✳

I marveled at the genius of Dr. Meyer's insight. He took me back to the city, and once again I was ready to take on the world. Sure enough, a few weeks later, I was completely refreshed and able to fall asleep as soon as my head hit the pillow.

Back in Vienna, life took on a renewed sense of excitement for me. I returned to the show, settled into a regular performance schedule, and spent my downtime hanging with the artists who, among other things, understood the "art" of living life to its fullest.

My relationship with Dr. Meyer grew more intense, and by the summer of 1970, the end of my first year in Vienna, I was completely in love with him. He was a truly enlightened man, and I loved living in the glow he emanated. The more time we spent together, the more I realized my ability to live in the present moment. I began to understand and enjoy his joie de vivre.

Dr. Meyer also had a unique insight into the power of music, a subject that held a great deal of interest to me. He'd once had an autistic patient whom nobody had been able to reach. Instead of giving up on her, as everyone else had, he'd taken a guitar into her room and played it for her. She'd responded immediately, and eventually he'd been able to make tremendous progress. Now, of course, music therapy is a common form of alternative treatment, but back then it was all but unheard-of. In that sense he was a true innovator in the melding of music and healing. His work in this field touched me deeply,

In the German production of *Godspell* in Hamburg, circa late 1960s–early 1970s. I'm making my Tweety Pie face.

Photographer unknown; photo courtesy of the Summer archives

Here I am in a promotional shot with the cast of the German production of *Godspell*. *Photographer unknown; photo courtesy of Helmuth Sommer*

right to the innermost sense of my faith, and made me believe that his pioneering vision was his gift from God.

Gradually it became clear that Dr. Meyer and I weren't really going anywhere *except* the present moment. I had to face the truth that marriage was a practical impossibility for us. Instead, I had cultivated yet another of my destined-to-be-lifelong friends. I remember the night we had a discussion about marriage, one I thought was vague enough not to sound like he was pushing anything. He looked at me, took my hand, and explained that he wanted to marry me, but felt I couldn't be happy staying in a small town like Vienna when the world was waiting for me. He didn't think we could be happy sacrificing one career for the other, and without total commitment, marriage between us didn't stand a chance of working.

After that night, we shifted away from a physical to a more platonic relationship. Even as we did, he continued to help me conquer my major fears—of being alone, of feeling abandoned, of believing I was unworthy. He was instrumental in helping me understand many of the phobias I still had.

Our romance was over, but not our friendship. Shortly thereafter I dated a director for about nine months and then broke it off. I dated some rich socialites, but that wasn't my style. I was careful not to fall in love again so soon. Then, in the midst of everything, I ran into Helmuth Sommer, a young, very blond actor from Vienna.

Helmuth and I had actually met each other a year earlier, when I'd briefly performed in the Berlin production of *Hair,* where he had been in the chorus. I was attracted to him then, but I let myself believe he was too young, too blond, and too in-nocent, right down to his big round blue eyes and cupid lips. He looked more like an angel than anything, and that somehow, initially at least, evoked a maternal rather than a sensual re-sponse in me. I remember watching him dance one night in Hamburg and thinking to myself how delicate, how ethereal he looked.

I hadn't seen him since we'd both left *Hair.* We started hanging around together, until he suddenly up and went to Greece for a year. Then, just as suddenly, a few days after I was cast as one of the leads of the Hamburg production of *The Me Nobody Knows,* Helmuth showed up, auditioned, and was cast.

He came to the casting call with a beautiful French girl on his arm who looked like Brigitte Bardot's double. He told me he had met her in Athens and had decided to bring her back with him. I told him how lucky he was to have a girl so beautiful and so obviously devoted. His response took me by surprise. With a shrug of his shoulders, he said he wasn't in love with her and that he was about to send her back to Paris.

During the next few weeks of rehearsals, our friendship grew, and I felt myself being drawn to him. One night a few weeks after we opened, I was sitting in my dressing room af-ter a performance feeling especially lonely when Helmuth knocked on my door. He wanted to know if I was up for some dancing. Why not, I thought to myself. I threw on some jeans and some makeup, and much to my surprise we had a great time. We then started going out after the show every night and became closer to each other than we had been before.

We completed the run of *The Me Nobody Knows* in Hamburg and did another show for the same company. That one took us to Switzerland. It was there, in the land of fine watches and sweet chocolate, that I finally fell for him. One night, we were out dancing at an after-hours club when a group of fellow actors bet me they could get Helmuth drunk. "No way," I said. "I know my best friend—he's not a drinker." Unfortunately (or maybe fortunately), Helmuth, who could not hold his liquor very well, soon got very drunk and very sick. I had to escort him back to his room, where he promptly started to throw up. I cleaned him up and put him in bed, at which point he sweetly asked if he could kiss me. I said no because he smelled like puke. With my sensitive nose, that would have been a hard memory to shake.

The next morning, I knocked on the door to see how he was doing. He said he was doing fine and then asked me in to listen to his new album from America. He turned on the stereo where he had Isaac Hayes's *Shaft* cued up, and reached for me yet again. He wasn't about to take no for an answer. I stared into his baby blue eyes, his draping blond hair, and his face of an angel. For the first time, I was powerless to resist him. He proved he was more than an angel. With the sound of *Shaft* pounding in my ears, almost as loud as the beating of my heart, we took a love ride. Becoming involved with Helmuth was a major surprise to me, but as we spent our evenings dancing and having fun with each other, we fell in love.

We then both joined the cast of *Godspell*, traveling throughout the German-speaking countries, and went on to do

On a walk through the Black Forest, circa late 1960s–early 1970s.

Photographer unknown; photo courtesy of Helmuth Sommer

a show called *The Black Experience* in Italy, a production that was extremely popular in the tourist resorts, but not with me. I didn't like anything about it. The production was poorly done, and the accommodations for the actors were terrible. When that show closed and we returned to Vienna, Helmuth asked me to marry him and, in 1972, I did just that.

✳

Believe me when I tell you that marriage was the last thing on my mind after Dr. Meyer. And yet, after more than four years of living in Europe and loving it, I somehow found myself married to the least likely man I'd dated. No matter, I told myself; I was determined to make my marriage work.

We moved back to Munich, where a few months later I discovered I was pregnant.

One day early in my pregnancy, I woke up feeling strangely sick and as if I were about to faint. Concerned, Helmuth rushed me to my doctor at the local hospital, where we discovered that I had nearly miscarried. The placenta was separating from the walls of my uterus, creating a serious threat to my pregnancy. My doctor then told me that if I wanted this baby, I'd have to lie on my back for the remaining six months of the pregnancy. It was critical to rest.

So off Helmuth and I went to stay at his parents' apartment in Vienna, just a six-hour drive from Munich. It was a beautiful apartment with high ceilings, big rooms, and ceramic tile fireplaces like they used to have in old castles. Helmuth's parents had wonderful Biedermeier furniture, French damask and brocades on the settee, and a superbly crafted, masterfully inlaid wooden dining table. Enormous windows spanned from the ceiling almost to the parquet floors. All of my aesthetic senses rejoiced. I was banished to what seemed to be paradise. My mind flashed to the antique stores I used to visit with my mother as a child, and I just couldn't get the smile off my face.

We stayed in Helmuth's parents' bedroom, as they were living full-time at their country home. His sister and her husband also shared the apartment with us. It was great to have company! The first few days in bed seemed like a little vacation after years of travel. But that soon wore off with the onslaught of enormous boredom, morning sickness, and eagerness to hold my baby. How was it I could feel so content and so bored at the same time? On the one hand I was surrounded by such beauty and, more importantly, about to become a mother. On the other hand, time moved too slowly. I read all the books I could in German and tried to increase my vocabulary. I read about the art of Austrian cuisine and learned a bit about wine and the art of living well.

One time when I was feeling strong, Helmuth snuck me out of the house and took me to the Schönbrunn Palace. It was autumn, and the trees were all changing colors. I stood in the middle of a pile of swirling leaves to recapture the first day I'd met God, in the schoolyard in Boston. We were able to walk into the gardens and sit on the grounds. It was a Monet. I felt refreshed. I was thousands of miles from my childhood and about to become a mother myself, yet I still felt just like a child inside. I wanted to get up and roll around in the fall leaves like I did

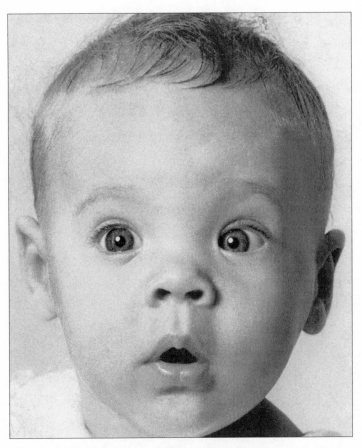

Mimi as a baby. *Photo courtesy of the Sudano family archives*

when I was a little girl at home in America. My home . . . America. Even that sounded so strange now.

The days grew shorter and shorter, and there was less and less light. Christmas came and went, and the new year dawned.

The time for my next doctor's appointment was drawing nigh, so we drove back to Munich from Vienna, and a friend of ours, Carl-Walter, let us stay in his furnished apartment in Munich. On February 16, 1973, Helmuth's birthday, at the Münchener Krankenhaus (the Munich Hospital) we embraced Mimi for the first time.

Mimi's birth was painful but fast. Midway through my labor they sedated me. All I can remember is the nurse saying, "Sit up, Frau Sommer. *Wollen Sie nicht ihre Baby sehen?*" I asked, "What is it?" The nurse said, "*Ist ein Mädchen.*" I had a girl! Tears rolled down my face. She had ten fingers, ten toes, black hair, blue eyes, and the "cutiest" little lips I had ever seen. I was officially a mother! Hallelujah! God is good! We had made it.

I looked back on my pregnancy and how I had prayed every day for this little person to make it. He had heard me pray. I knew then, just as I know now, that God is real.

6

Munich Madness

Motherhood was joyful. It completely changed my life and my world. For the first time in years, my focus was not completely on me, and to my surprise, I found that to be a wonderful thing—at least in the beginning. For the first few months after giving birth, I didn't work, I didn't go out at night, and I didn't do anything but care for this beautiful blue-eyed angel baby who looked just like her daddy. However, as time passed I began to feel lonely and isolated.

After a while I began to miss the fun and excitement of performing. That longing triggered my discontent. I began to wonder if I was simply not good enough to be on the stage. Maybe I had gotten married and had a baby as a convenient excuse to avoid failure? These feelings and thoughts eventually led me to reevaluate my marriage. It felt like a steel lock had been put on the most important door of my life, a door that had taken me a long time to pry open. I never stopped to consider that having a child might actually be the opening of yet another, more important door, which of course it was. Unfortunately, I didn't realize this while stuck in a small apartment with a little baby and a husband who worked most of the time. As a result, I fell into a major depression.

Helmuth was a doll, always helpful and encouraging. He had a wonderful spirit. The problem in our relationship was me—I just wasn't ready for the nonstop responsibility of marriage and parenthood. I was emotionally immature.

In the midst of all this, Dr. Meyer called to say that he would soon pay me a visit. I hadn't seen him for a while and was looking forward to his arrival. After we'd spent a few minutes together he took a deep breath and declared that he'd always known I would sacrifice my career and settle for second best. He was the one man who had relentlessly pushed me to reach for the outer limits of my abilities. I'd thought he believed in me. I was devastated at his comments. He was my mentor. His cynical words drove me even deeper into depression.

The only people I felt I could turn to were my girlfriend Anna, from the original Munich production of *Hair,* and Carl-Walter, Mimi's godfather. I think Anna felt sorry for me because I appeared so unprepared for motherhood. She would come over and show me how to do things like fold diapers. She also taught me how to get Mimi to sleep through the night. (My little darling was one of those babies who woke up just after midnight and wailed an aria or two for a couple of hours.) Anna's secret was to bathe Mimi right before bedtime, not to feed her when she woke up, and to make sure the last bottle or food at night didn't give her gas. Everything she told me turned out to be right. Her care and kindness toward me was crucial, and I soon found myself sharing all my woes with her.

By the fall of 1973, I had become extremely tense and fearful. I had an extended postpartum depression, and my insomnia, along with the rest of my phobias, had returned. I became paranoid and frightened and often felt faint. I finally realized I needed an outlet. I needed to get out of the house and sing. I joined a local pop group called the Family Tree. It was more than a bit humbling, because for the first time ever I wasn't the lead singer.

There were twelve singers and soloists in the group. One sang well, but the others were frequently off-key. Not that it mattered; they knew how to entertain, and the audiences seemed to love them. I didn't stay with the Family Tree for very long, but at least it got me back on the stage long enough to give me the courage to try to put together my own one-woman show.

On the nights I wasn't performing with the group or rehearsing, I'd take Mimi over to Anna's house and hang out. On one of those nights I became reacquainted with Gunther, a married man I'd met years ago. Tall with light brown hair, he was a model-cum-artiste. What a small world, I told myself, with the same circle of characters continually reappearing—and, in the case of Gunther, at the most opportune time. He was interesting and challenging, not necessarily romantic. He seemed to be a wild man in the way he spoke and the way he moved. He was all male, alpha male. Though he was a painter, I think he had all the attributes of a rock 'n' roll musician. Gunther commanded any room he entered. Beyond his personal magnetism, he was as mysterious as the man that "rode in on a horse with no name." I would be out and about, in my daily café jaunts, and I'd run into Gunther. Eventually our casual acquaintance would turn into something much more intense. I could see Gunther peering across the chasm of our circumstances, and I would catch glimpses of his longing. It was clear he had a deep desire to partake of this forbidden fruit. It is amazing how deceptive the staring eyes of a needy soul can be.

His good looks and artwork had intrigued me and reignited my interest in art. I began to spend hours analyzing his paintings. He was always amazed at my intuitive ability to "think and see" things abstractly. With Gunther's constant encouragement, I felt a gradual reawakening of my creative spirit, and inspired by his art, I began taking my own brushes back out.

They say still waters run deep, and I could sense there was a raging current beneath his surface. I felt myself tempted to ride the rapids into his dangerous and uncharted waters. "I found someone . . . my first . . . my last . . . my everything"—these lyrics haunted me! The sounds of Barry White filled the air.

This is not to say that Gunther didn't have an enormous ego and an obvious "crazy artist" component to his personality. He did, and I knew it. My understanding of his allegedly twisted childhood was, however, under the circumstances, deeply compelling. His dark side only made him more attractive to me. His inner sadness drew me in. His mother was a somewhat successful actress who had abandoned his upbringing to the headmasters of boarding schools or his aunt so that she could enjoy her artistic endeavors. His father was either long gone or dead. Gunther had grown up alone, feeling unwanted. He carried his unresolved feelings about his mother into every relationship he ever had. He was needy, and I was, by nature, the caretaker of lost souls. My ability to nurture made him even more dependent on me than either of us knew, and at the time, I liked that very, very much. I needed to feel needed, and I mistook his neurotic needs for the passion of true love.

But there *was* that dark side. Gunther was married and had a tumultuous on-and-off relationship with his wife, with a history of violence toward her. Whenever he couldn't control her, his insecurities would manifest themselves in excessive drinking and physical abuse. He would ultimately apologize and suffer intense bouts of self-pity, self-deprivation, and shame. Nevertheless, Gunther and his wife grew more and more estranged.

I was besieged by my own inner darkness. I was struggling with deep depression and overwhelming thoughts of suicide. I felt trapped. It seemed that my husband, Helmuth, didn't care enough about me. All he did was work night after night, and sleep all day. I constantly pleaded with him to spend more time at home with me and our baby. I was oppressed by loneliness. I became afraid to be home alone in the house with my baby, though she was the one and only spark of light in that darkness.

Shortly before Christmas, Helmuth and I decided to try a trial separation, and I went to Anna's to get away from Helmuth and our apartment. This offered me an opportunity to hear other voices, human voices that, thankfully, were louder than the tormenting voices in my own head. Gunther would drop by on occasion to visit Anna's husband, his best friend. We were both at home in Anna's house, giving us the connection that would lead us soon to common ground. I had a sense we were fellow travelers, searching for each other. What a desperate duo we were, perfect for each other. At least, for the time being.

Then it happened. One night, while I was there alone at Anna's with Mimi, having just put her to sleep, Gunther showed up unexpectedly and we started discussing our marital problems. He recognized my high level of anxiety and coerced me to take a couple of sips of wine. I fell prey to Gunther's illustrious seduction that night.

I knew in my heart and soul that I had crossed the uncrossable line. I recognized the demise of my own moral convictions, and it shook the very foundation of my emotional stability. What did God think of me now? I shuddered at the idea that my eternal options were narrowing. What would Helmuth think of me? I knew my life was transparent in God's eyes, but how could I continue to deceive Helmuth? Could I trust my husband to forgive me when I couldn't even forgive myself? Gunther, on the other hand, flourished because of my emotional turmoil and now wanted to possess me *at any cost*. He stepped up his pursuit of me to the point of what would be described today as stalking. This, oddly, enticed and excited me—I was drawn to his burning need as much as he was to me.

Shortly thereafter, I went to the town of Knokke, Belgium, on a singing engagement without Helmuth. Overcome by loneliness, I stupidly decided to pen a steamy love letter to Gunther.

I disguised myself by signing the letter "Love, Paul." After reading the letter, Gunther placed it in his desk drawer, where it was found later that day by his wife. Believing that she had discovered that his secret life was the real reason for Gunther's abuse and the cause of their estrangement, she decided to take the letter with her to a local club and show it around. It just so happened that night to be the same club where Helmuth worked as the headwaiter.

Helmuth, drawn to all the commotion, caught a glimpse of the letter and did a double take. The handwriting appeared disturbingly familiar as he read the words:

Missing you deeply here in Knokke.
Love, Paul

Was this Donna's handwriting? he wondered. The very thought made him feel as if he'd been stabbed in the heart. He asked quietly, *"Dauf ich das im Licht sehen, bitte?"* May I see it in the light, please?

Upon my return from Knokke, Helmuth confronted me. He told me he had seen "the letter." I knew immediately that he knew the truth, and squirm as I might, there was no way out. I could see the pain in his eyes as he wrestled with the concept of my being unfaithful. How could someone he held so high stoop so low? I was completely unable to deal with the situation. He was broken, and so was I.

Not long after, feeling I could never repair the breach of trust, I made one of the most difficult decisions of my life. I knew I had to leave Helmuth. Not because of Gunther, but because of the calling I had to pursue—because of my singing. Helmuth told me that if there was music there in my heart, he would let me go.

Gunther stood by me during the first difficult days of my separation from Helmuth, and whenever I started to weaken, he encouraged me to keep my focus on my calling. This setting was perfect for Gunther, and as the saying goes, when he was good he was *very* good. During this time Gunther became my major crutch. He lavished his most sensitive, kind, and humane qualities on me. Gunther took Mimi and me on wonderful rides in the country and made paintings of me, but more than anything, he stood by my side and nurtured me back to emotional health, through the inevitable depression that goes with self-induced failure. I was powerless to resist him, yet at the same time I was extremely afraid of being controlled by him.

Unfortunately, when Gunther was bad, he was horrible. As I became more secure, he became more insecure and would compensate by drinking heavily. Because of his alcohol-fueled temper, I tried my best to keep an emotional arm's length from him, which made for a stormy on-again, off-again relationship. One night Gunther and I went out to a club with some friends. At one point I was walking across the dance floor and a man grabbed my hand and asked if he could dance with me. I politely declined and walked back to our table. The man from the dance floor followed me back to the table and sat down across from me, in Gunther's empty seat. He asked, "Is that your drink?" "Yes," I said. He picked up my drink and drank right out of it! He then reached for my hand again and tried to pull me onto the dance floor. I said no, this time a bit louder. Just then Gunther appeared. Seeing the man harassing me, Gunther raced over to me and grabbed the guy. He punched him, sat him down, picked him up again, punched him, sat him down again, and then kicked his chair, which was on rollers, all the way to the door and down the flight of stairs that led to the street. I stared in total disbelief. Gunther was indeed a dangerous man.

I was terrified of his violent temper! I couldn't believe what he had done. It's true the fellow had been out of line, but Gunther's reaction was completely way over the top. Somehow he avoided going to jail, and in retrospect, that only made him worse.

Sometimes he did things I couldn't stand. He would sleep with other women just to try to make me jealous, but his childish behavior didn't faze me in the least. He'd come back, confess everything, and say he was sorry. It didn't matter to me. I was unaffected by his behavior. My attitude would make him so crazy he'd go off, drink, and get even crazier. There were times I tried to leave him, and that's when I learned firsthand what it felt like to be on the receiving end of his uncontrollable violence. One night he literally kicked the bathroom door off its frame trying to get to me. Another time I came home and found him enraged over something completely trivial. All six foot four of him slapped the five foot eight of me around and then threw me across the room, straight into my glass cabinet. Pieces of glass pierced my skin and scalp. I had glass in my hair, my face, and all over my body.

When I finally could get up I called the police, who warned him to stay away from me. Despite their warnings, he just kept coming around. He tried to get us back together. He told everyone that "our trouble" was really all my fault. He claimed I had become too arrogant and full of myself, and that I had kicked him out for no reason. In other words, he wanted everyone to think that *he* was the victim!

Including me.

Even after he began to abuse me, my insecurities led me to believe that I had destroyed my marriage because of this man and that therefore somehow I had to stick it out. Besides that, I figured I must have done something to provoke him. Maybe I shouldn't have said this, maybe I shouldn't have done that. I started playing that head game because as dangerous as it was to be with him, I really didn't want to face the alternative of "being alone." Here we were, two lost souls, groping at each other in mutual darkness. What a mess; what an utterly hopeless mess.

I kept myself busy and picked up singing work wherever I could. One day, a friend of mine told me about a producer who was looking for new voices. Maybe he could use me. It wasn't what I wanted, but it was a job. I set up an appointment to meet the man.

That man turned out to be Giorgio Moroder.

7

Love to Love You Baby

Giorgio and I took to each other right away. He was a young, hustling record producer and composer who'd had a string of notable hits in Germany and America with the kind of elementary, singsong type of Top 40 tunes that were so popular at the time. Like me, he was a foreigner, having been born in Italy; he'd moved to Germany when it became clear that Munich was the creative hub of the new Europe, especially for music. Several of the artists who would come to dominate rock 'n' roll in the sixties and seventies got their start in Germany, most notably the Beatles.

Giorgio had been a performer in his teens, playing in a band that toured Europe, which was how he'd discovered the Munich music scene. In 1967 he left the road and put all his focus into songwriting. He set up shop in Berlin and scored a couple of quick hits with Michael Holm and Ricky Shane, but he didn't quite find the sound for which he was searching. He moved to Munich in '71 and set up his own studio, Musicland, where he hoped to create new music to feed his own label. Working with his partner, Pete Bellotte, Giorgio was constantly looking for new voices to use on the endless stream of demos he churned out.

Giorgio was very intense. He had dark curly hair, a thick mustache that drooped like an Italian gunman's in a spaghetti Western, and eyes that could illuminate a sheet of music without a flashlight.

That first day he asked me to sing something, and I did a few numbers from *Hair*. He liked what he heard and asked if I knew anything else. I went through a couple of other show tunes that I'd been doing for a while. When I finished he said he thought my singing was good enough for him to work with.

After that, I returned to Giorgio's studio every day, running through endless songs and arrangements that he and Pete had created. He was looking for a special sound and thought I had the ability to give it to him. As a result, he became my teacher as well as my creative mentor, and with his encouragement, my singing ability grew in a new and exciting way.

One of the most important aspects of my singing that Giorgio encouraged me to expand was my approach to a song. To this day I will approach a song as an actress approaches a script. I do not sing; I act. When I sing, I sing with the voice of the character in the song. Because of that, I don't have to make every song something from my perspective; rather, it's something from the heart and the soul of the character who is doing the singing. At a time in pop music when everyone on the charts sounded more or less the same, when radio tunes were coming out of their pseudo-psychedelic phase and reverting to a more blandly generic Tin Pan Alley sound, both Giorgio and I wanted to do something different and capture it on record. We were looking to create a sound and a singing style based less on the tradition of the jukebox and more on that of the theater. My greatest gift as a singer-songwriter has always been telling stories. That's why I was a natural for musical theater. And it is what first caught the eye, ear, and imagination of Giorgio.

From the beginning, I loved Giorgio's personal, soft-spoken, but intense style and his creative methods. I sensed right away that he was a true original and that his music had the potential for greatness. He was a master behind the console. Along with Pete, he could do simplicity as easily as he could do grandeur, all with a marvelously unerring ear for production.

Giorgio's home and offices were located near the airport at the Arrabella House in Munich, just outside the city proper. Beneath the building was his recording studio, which is where he recorded his demos.

The timing for my meeting Giorgio couldn't have been any better. Having left Helmuth and being unsure of Gunther's stability meant I was going to have to raise Mimi by myself. I needed to make some real money. I thought working with Giorgio would provide Mimi and me with some much needed cash.

Giorgio was constantly recording, demoing and cataloging his own songs. If someone came to him needing a song, he'd

Christmas with Mimi. *Photo by Helmuth Sommer*

have not one but ten for them to choose from, already recorded the way he wanted them to sound.

The first demos I sang were for Three Dog Night, a group in America that Giorgio was pitching to. They were trying to develop a slightly more sophisticated sound above the bubblegum they had gotten their creative shoes stuck on.

Giorgio not only was totally supportive in the studio but took a personal interest in me and saw to it that I got back on my own two feet. With his moral and financial support, Mimi and I were able to move into a new apartment, away from the constant threat of Gunther's volatility, which loomed over my every waking moment. Those were difficult times for me. I felt as if I were trapped in a long, dark, windowless corridor in which there was just one door that led to the light. Dear Giorgio held open that door.

I had already developed a minor reputation in Germany as a pop singer. By the time I started working with Giorgio, I had recorded several songs from the musicals I had been in that had become hits.

Giorgio had written a *schlaga* tune called "The Hostage" that he was going to record when the 1972 Olympic tragedy happened, after which no one in Germany would touch it. *Schlaga* is a type of bubblegum music that was very popular in Germany during the late sixties and early seventies. It was very similar to the Archies hit "Sugar, Sugar," only in the German language.

Despite its title, "The Hostage" had nothing to do with politics. It's actually written in the form of a morbid phone call from a husband to his wife. Not exactly the stuff of American Top 40, but we recorded it in 1973, and, thankfully, it got picked up by Holland television and became a Top Ten hit.

Recording these songs for Giorgio helped bring me back to music and back to life. I had been out of the public and private spotlight for too long, and now I was eager to get reacquainted with both. Having settled into my new digs, I wasted no time. On weekends I would travel to Holland to make live appearances; for some bizarre reason, our recording of "The Hostage" was very popular there. Every promoter wanted to book me into the local clubs so people could hear and see me sing the song. Every Friday afternoon I'd leave Germany, where I was less well known, and travel across the border by train to Holland, where a huge entourage waited for me. Talk about a strange dichotomy.

After "The Hostage" we made a series of recordings, beginning with "Lady of the Night," that were completely different from anything and everything I'd ever done or even heard before. I like to think of that time as musical boot camp. Oy!

We followed "Lady of the Night" with "Denver Dreams" and "Virgin Mary," the lyrics of which were more or less the same as the first two, a bit melodramatic with a tilt toward the schlocky side of life. These recordings were invaluable, as they gave Giorgio and me a chance to develop our creative relationship. We would cut these songs again and again until I was able to sing them just the way Giorgio heard them in his head.

Working with Giorgio was a priceless opportunity for me to learn the craft of three-minute, maximize-the-lyrics, maximize-the-hook pop songwriting. It was through Giorgio's teachings that I began to understand how to write radio-ready tunes that got across exactly what I wanted to say. Billy Joel, Stevie Wonder, Marvin Gaye, Paul Simon, Paul McCartney, and Elton John are masters of this songwriting approach.

Early in 1975 I had been playing around with a song idea. I didn't have anything more than just the title. In fact, the line was originally written as "I'd love to love you," which I thought was so cool. When I gave it to Giorgio he paused for a second and then said, excitedly, "Donna! I like this!" He walked around the studio looking like a mad scientist from some B horror movie as he moved his hands to a silent recording he could already hear in his head.

I went home at the end of that day and didn't think any more about the song until the next morning, when, first thing, there was a knock on my door. It was Giorgio's girlfriend, Helga. Poor Helga, she could have called me but I didn't have a phone, which is why he'd sent her to wake me up. She said he *needed* to see me "right now."

By the time I got there, Giorgio was ready to lay down the first track of the song that he'd worked on through the night, building it around my title. I remember standing in the studio sipping a cup of much needed herbal tea as Giorgio kept asking me how I wanted to sing it. I kept telling him I didn't know, so we worked on it together for a while, and I decided to give it a try. My goal was to capture on record the sound Giorgio heard in his head. How I did that gets at the heart of how and why I sing.

I believe that people have first, second, and third talents.

The trick is to understand what your first talent is, because that is the one from which all the others will follow and be released. Through my years of performing onstage in Europe I was certain my first talent was singing, followed closely by writing and acting. These last two often go with singing, because in order to perform a song successfully an artist needs to be able to evoke the emotion.

Sometimes it takes a while for me to discover who the character in a song is, and sometimes I nail it right away. With "Love to Love You Baby," I came up with an image of Marilyn Monroe singing the song in that light and fluffy but highly sensual voice of hers, and hers was the image I used when I laid down the first vocal track for the song. That would be the only track we did that day. *"Perfetto!"* Giorgio cried when I finished. Before noon we had the vocal for the record down cold.

What happened next came as a complete surprise to me. Giorgio was so excited about "Love to Love You Baby" (as the lyric and title had become), that he took the song with him that January to MIDEM, an international music convention. MIDEM is the music industry's equivalent to the Cannes Film Festival. While there he met Neil Bogart of Casablanca Records and told him he had something special. Talk about the hand of fate!

Neil Bogart was a Brooklyn-born kid with a rock 'n' roll dream. While still a teenager he'd worked as a song-and-dance man on cruise ships before cutting a single, "Bobby," at the age of eighteen. "Bobby" became a surprise hit that added Neil to the endless list of pop's one-hit wonders. Still, his three minutes of fame had been long enough to hook him into show business.

Hip enough to know he wasn't good enough to be the next Bobby Darin (who was?), Neil took a position with *CashBox* magazine and soon after was hired by MGM Records as a promotion man—the perfect job for the perfect self-promoter. He then quickly moved himself over to the Philadelphia-based Cameo Records, where he became vice president and sales manager. In the early sixties Cameo was bought out by Allen Klein, one of the new breed of "killer" rock 'n' roll managers whose roster included, among others, the Rolling Stones. Klein and Neil did not get along. Neil left the company to help start a new label called Buddah Records. By the age of twenty-four, Neil was a seasoned music-industry veteran and Buddah was cranking out hit after hit.

Neil found a successful formula at Buddah, which quickly became the reigning label for "bubblegum." Their roster included the very successful 1910 Fruitgum Company and the Brooklyn Bridge. Neil rightly tagged bubblegum as the perfect bridge between sixties rock and seventies club music, which was soon to give way to the pulsating beat of disco.

Buddah lasted about five years, until 1973, when the bubblegum sound finally lost its flavor (pun intended). Looking to make a bold new move, Neil struck a deal with Mo Ostin, then head of Warner Records, to bankroll and distribute a new label, Casablanca. Neil had originally wanted to call the label Emerald City Records, after one of his favorite movies, *The Wizard of Oz,* but when he discovered that the name was already taken, he shifted to another favorite flick, *Casablanca,* starring Humphrey Bogart, a name with strong recognition.

The first major act Neil signed to Casablanca was Kiss, who became a monster hit and catapulted the label to the top of the charts. As happens so many times, success nearly killed Casablanca. Their expenses ramped up, and a follow-up hit group proved hard to find. Partly out of inspiration and partly out of desperation, Neil put together a novelty record of comedy clips, titled *Here's Johnny: Magic Moments from "The Tonight Show,"* and did something no one else had ever done. As the story goes, he put the label's entire advertising budget, a million and a half dollars, into TV ads to promote this one album. The record was only a moderate success, with enough sales to keep Neil in business while he continued to search for the Next Big Thing.

In January 1975, Neil went to MIDEM looking for just that. Giorgio told Neil he had just what he was looking for and gave him a copy of our demo for "Love to Love You Baby." I was amazed when Giorgio came back from MIDEM with the news that there was interest in our record.

Neil took the record back home to America and played it during a party. His friends kept asking him to play it over and over. Still later that night, alone with his wife, he put it on as background music while they made love. The next day he called Giorgio in Munich and told him he loved the record and he had a great idea for promoting it. He asked Giorgio to expand the original three-minute track to seventeen minutes, to fill an entire side, the perfect amount of time to "get the job done." Do that, he told Giorgio, and he would release it as one side of a dance album instead of just a single. Giorgio tried to explain to Neil that all we had done was cut the demo. "I'll need to find the right singer for the actual release," Giorgio said. Neil cried, "No, no, no! Whoever is on that demo is the only one who can sing that song. It's the voice you want to take home and make love to!"

Giorgio called me to come back into the studio to expand the song by adding fourteen minutes. "Fourteen minutes? That's an awful lot of lyrics," I said.

"Don't worry—we'll improvise. Make it sound sexy," Giorgio said. That's when we dimmed the lights, lit a few candles, and I added all those oohs and aahs. You see, I'd never intended to sing the song that way. I'd only intended to give Giorgio my idea for the song. When it came time to expand it to seventeen minutes, Giorgio left all those oohs and aahs in because the song didn't have any more words!

Sometimes magic happens when you're just trying to figure out how to get the rabbit into the hat in the first place. The sound that became world famous, the seductive moans and groans of "Love to Love You Baby," happened simply because we had run out of words, and I had to do something to fill up the time.

When it was through, all anyone ever wanted to know was where that rabbit had come from!

Upon its release, "Love to Love You Baby" became an immediate, international symbol of . . . *something,* although I've never been quite sure of what. It was certainly more than just another sexy song, and it went on to become the anthem of seventies pop culture.

Or so they tell me.

✳

Much to my amazement, "Love to Love You Baby" was a huge hit in America, despite the fact that the song had little airplay and no one had any idea who I was. (It didn't help that I lived in Munich.) Most program directors considered the album version too long and too racy. However, Frankie Crocker, a New York City deejay at WBLS radio, loved the song and decided to play the extended version every night after midnight. Prior to that sales had come primarily from club play. Neil told Giorgio that I had to come to the States to promote the song on the radio to send sales into the stratosphere.

Believe it or not, this was not good news to me. I had been living in Europe for seven years and had never felt the need to return to America. While I loved the United States and my family was there, to me going home represented a step backward in my life. I'd never thought walking back over burned bridges was a very smart idea. And I was still afraid I might encounter retaliation from my teenage experience in Boston.

However, since the call had come from Neil, and Giorgio agreed with him, I knew I was going to have to go, no matter how difficult it was going to be to leave my physical, creative, and spiritual home, not to mention the friends I'd made, who had become my "chosen" family.

I strongly believe that the physical is related to the emotional (and vice versa), which is why I was not surprised when, a few weeks before I was scheduled to leave Germany, I developed a serious heart condition that almost killed me. Gunther and I went to Switzerland to see a friend who was in a show. The next night, on our way back home, somewhere in the region of the Black Forest, we pulled into a rest stop. I opened my door and suddenly found myself unable to breathe. I collapsed and fell out of the car onto the pavement. And out of nowhere, within minutes, a police car appeared and took me, unconscious, to a hospital in the Black Forest that specialized in heart conditions.

Talk about a miracle! It was the one facility in all of Germany that could have helped me in the condition I was in. Fortunately for me, we were only five minutes away from it.

I was confined there for a month, denied all visitors, including my daughter (who was being cared for by Roberta Kelly, a friend of mine and a fellow singer), and permitted no access to television, phone, books, or radio. Nothing. Just silence. The only thing I could do was look out the window from my private room into the woods. What a metaphor for the dilemma I now found myself in.

My life had suddenly come to one of those places where in order to survive you have to walk a tightrope over the highest canyons in the world with no net. At that moment I had very shaky feet and the pulse of an eighty-year-old person.

This was it and I had to keep myself sane while I tried to recover. I kept telling myself that God was there with me, that He knew I was going to pull through, and that He just wanted to make sure I was strong enough to handle all that lay ahead. After all, what's not battened down can be shaken. I had done some things during my years in Europe that I wasn't proud of, including my marital infidelity. There were times when I'd fallen out of sync with my spiritual self, and I felt that now I was paying the price. The many ways I had demeaned and demoralized my soul came crashing down on me, pushing me to the ground and landing me on the edge of my life. I prayed to God for His forgiveness and His guidance.

It was the most difficult time I'd ever gone through. Finally, after four weeks that seemed like four years, I turned the corner and began the slow road to recovery. I had developed a serious case of myocarditis, an infection of the heart muscle and membrane. Apparently, I'd gotten the infection from nose drops that I had been using for allergies for more than a year; unbeknownst to me, they weren't supposed to be used for more than three days at a time. This had had a weakening effect on my heart, although it was probably more complicated than that.

When I was finally released, I was warned—ordered was more like it—by the doctors to stay in bed for another entire month, *or else* I would almost certainly suffer a relapse that could be fatal. Gunther took me home, and I did just as I was told. I stayed in bed for another month, and he attended to my every need.

✳

Having been bedridden for those weeks, I was nearly out of money. Even though it still felt too early for me to even think about work, I took a gig on a two-week cruise, hoping the sea air would reinvigorate me. Just before I embarked, I decided to visit my doctor to make absolutely sure it was okay for me to go back to singing. Not excited about the prospect, he made me promise I wouldn't work too hard, then gave me his qualified approval to take the job.

The next day I boarded the ship. I had scarcely unpacked my bags when I got sick all over again, and I spent nearly the entire cruise in bed. By the time we returned I was *barely* able to crawl back to my apartment in Munich. It was going to take me more time to heal.

Despite my precarious physical condition, Neil had kept pushing Giorgio to get me to America to promote "Love to Love You Baby." The three-minute version was starting to get some airplay, and he was convinced that with the right promotion it would be a monster hit single, make us tons of money, and turn me into the newest, hottest recording star. I had barely enough time to unpack my bags from the cruise before I had to pack them again, this time for the big trip back to the States.

I had put off returning to America for as long as I could, until I felt strong enough to make the trip, and I hoped that I had at last conquered the bug that had almost killed me. I quickly realized that shuttling back and forth across the Atlantic would become impractical. My daughter, Mimi, was about to start preschool, and I didn't want to be any more of an absentee mother than necessary. Because of my recent hospitalization, she'd been through enough already. Anyway, if I was going to promote my song, I didn't want to do a halfhearted, "wham bam thank you, ma'am, I'm outta here" job. No, I was in tune with Neil's and Giorgio's thinking: *in for a penny, in for a gold record.*

And so, after several years' run in Munich, I decided to move back to America.

During the long hours of that flight I thought about all the things that had happened to me those past nearly eight years. I had learned a lot from many wonderful people and in doing so had acquired a backstage pass to the main event, my own life.

The frightened, sad little girl with the scarred face who'd left America with lots of ability but lots of doubt was returning a grown woman, one whose star was undeniably on the rise.

8

Stardom in America

My plane landed in New York City on a brisk November afternoon in 1975, and within my first hour back I felt that something special was in the air. I can pinpoint the exact moment everything changed for me. Giorgio and I had gone through customs and were met by Susan Munao, the head of publicity and artist relations for Casablanca Records. Susan and I jumped into the back of a stretch limo, the likes of which I'd never seen. As the driver started the engine, the radio came on, and miraculously, out of his speakers came the bass line of "Love to Love You Baby." At first I thought it must be an eight-track, "a nice touch" (and very Neil), but I soon realized it was a local radio station. When the music ended, a deejay came on and identified the song and mentioned my name. I turned to Susan in disbelief and saw that she was just as surprised as I was. We both screamed at the same time, so loud the driver almost went off the road! I was thrilled! What a great way to start.

In L.A., circa 1975, on my first promo tour. *Photo by Dagmar*

We drove to Central Park South, to New York City's Park Lane Hotel, and were ushered up to a suite overlooking the park. As I walked in, to my utter amazement, I noticed more than twenty floral arrangements spread throughout the huge suite. I thought I was in the wrong room, and as I started to turn around, Neil Bogart came up from behind me and pushed me back into the room. This was my warm Casablanca "Welcome to America."

I spent two days in that suite before I realized that all the flower arrangements were *not* part of the hotel's decor. Finally Susan told me they were for me and to open the note cards. This was the beginning of the new and wonderful "diva-licious" world into which I had surprisingly been ushered.

Before I had left for America, Giorgio had taken me on an extensive shopping spree, under Susan's explicit direction and warning *not* to show up without that *Love to Love You Baby* album cover dress, designed by Bill Gibb. Little did she know, we'd only leased the dress for the pictures and didn't own it. Giorgio and I were in a mad rush to find and purchase that dress!

Casablanca was slowly but surely beginning to transform the ordinary Donna Gaines, onetime hippie of Greenwich Village, into the uptown sophisticated diva Donna Summer. Even my name was changed from Sommer to Summer as part of my makeover. From being dressed to the nines in a full-length borrowed white mink coat over that *now* famous dress I finally owned to the hiring of top makeup artists and hairstylists from New York's fashion mecca, I was ready for my American debut at one of New York's hottest dance clubs, the Pachyderm. All this for me? Wow.

Besides the extravagant party at the Pachyderm, Neil, Joyce Biawitz (who later became my first manager), and Susan had arranged an amazing surprise. In promoting me and my album they'd brought a little California to New York in the most unique way. A hand-painted, life-sized cake made in my image by the famous Hansen's bakery had been transported to the Los Angeles Airport via an ambulance, boarded into two first-class seats, and chaperoned all the way across the country by Buck Reingold, the head of Casablanca's promotion department. In addition, my mother and father and family had been flown in from Boston to be a part of this incredible experience.

A picture I'll never forget was seeing my mother and father sitting in front of that enormous cake staring at the image of me from the back-cover photo of *Love to Love You Baby*. To me it seemed everything was "a piece of cake" for Neil and Susan.

I was about to embark on a massive American promotion and press tour. Over the next six weeks, I'd travel from New York to the West Coast with Susan and Cecil Holmes, vice president of Casablanca and Neil's partner.

I spent my first few days in New York City and then headed up to Boston with Susan and Cecil to see my family again. We were met by Casablanca's local promotion man, Brian Interland, who took me to one of the top radio stations in Boston to meet the famous deejay Sonny Joe White. I was excited to be back home. But, being a cautious person, I was also nervous. I had to find out what had happened to the boys that I

At the Pierre hotel in New York, circa 1975, my parents pose with the infamous *Love to Love You Baby* cake. It had been flown in from Hansen's Cakes in L.A. and brought to the hotel by ambulance. *Photo by Dagmar*

had helped send to prison all those years before. I discovered they had all been released from jail, had gone back into their violent way of life, and had all subsequently been killed in unrelated incidents. That was it. Although I felt truly sorry to hear what had happened, I thought to myself, "Thank God." I could finally be home with no fears from the past hanging over my head.

After having been away for so long, I loved seeing my whole extended family and my childhood friends. Being smothered by my family's hugs and kisses warmed me from head to toe. My father hugged me so hard I thought he was going to break my ribs!

I stayed at Boston's Copley Square Hotel for about a week, stretching my visit up until the last possible moment before I had to begin a grueling schedule of personal appearances all across America. My friend Roberta Kelly and her mother had watched Mimi when I'd traveled throughout Europe and could not take her along. Now, before I left, my mother and father offered to look after Mimi when I was on the road. I was grateful for their offer and quickly accepted. If there was one place I knew Mimi would be safe, well cared for, and loved, it was with my parents.

I set about crisscrossing America to promote the record, a schedule that kept me going nonstop as "Love to Love You Baby" turned into the hottest club song in the country. In fact, the club-based demand gave Neil the leverage to finally get the long form of the song on radio during the late-night listening hours.

Me with a rose in Boston on my first promo tour. I'm wearing the *Love to Love You Baby* dress. My sister Jeanette is in the foreground.

Photo by Dagmar

During those six long weeks on the road, Susan, Cecil, and I were so exhausted as we traveled from one city to another that we would often catnap on each other's shoulders. Thank God they were with me throughout that relentless schedule.

By now Susan Munao and I had spent a lot of time together. She is a brunette, pretty, petite, and straight from the streets of Brooklyn. A lioness in a Chihuahua's body is the image that comes to mind. She is of Italian descent, but swearing was her mother tongue and English her second language. Divorced and on her own, she threw herself into my career. She had moved to California to join Neil in September 1975 and had played a major role in helping create both the image of Casablanca Records and many of its artists. She worked every angle there was to promote the record and me.

The long weeks on the road culminated with my arrival at Casablanca's offices in Los Angeles. For the first time I was able to meet all the amazing staff members at Casablanca who'd been instrumental in helping with the album. I'd had no idea how many people worked behind the scenes, particularly Bruce Bird, Larry Harris, Maury Lathouwer, Mark Paul Simon, and Alice Gellis Harris, our special-events planner, to name only a few. But more importantly, there was Neil. It remains a testament to Neil's marketing genius that he was able to convince as many FM stations as he did to play the long version, after which Top 40 stations ultimately added the shortened version to their programming as their "pick hit of the week." His vision paid off, and we were presented with our first gold album.

All of this happened so fast it seemed unreal to me. Not

three months earlier I had been bedridden in a strange and lonely hospital in Europe, and now here I was back in America, promoting a demo that had somehow burned its way to the top of the charts.

The relentlessness of the tour schedule eventually caught up with me and took its toll. More than once I had to check into a hospital to recuperate from complete exhaustion. I feared that my heart condition might resurface. Neil understood and tried to make things as comfortable for me as he could. He always made sure there were plenty of people to take care of all my personal needs—hairstylists, costumers, scheduling assistants, and some of the top musicians, bandleaders, and choreographers in the business.

But he also wanted the best possible show, even if I was on the verge of collapse. He insisted on having a lot of dancers in the show to take some of the pressure off me, which was unconventional at the time for the average pop act. And at the center of it all was me, a human jukebox providing automatic live disco music on every dance floor, large or small, I could fit into my nonstop schedule. In Neil's way of thinking there were no little clubs . . . all clubs were important.

One example typical of the craziness that surrounded the record's popularity was a drag-show performer who decided to use "Love to Love You Baby" as his theme song. No sooner did he go on the road with his show than a rumor began that Donna Summer was actually a male transvestite! I thought it was funny. My mother happened to be listening to the radio one day and heard some talk show where a guest was saying that I was

In the *Love to Love You Baby* dress during a performance somewhere in New York, circa 1975. *Photo by Dagmar*

really a man. She got so incensed she called the station and started yelling at the deejay on the air, saying that her daughter was one hundred percent female, and she should know since she'd happened to be at the birth! I howled when I heard the story.

The next summer, "Love to Love You Baby" went to number one in South America and Italy. In the midst of my U.S. tour, Neil decided to send me to both places to help keep the record at the top of the charts. It was fun, but sometimes it was a bit terrifying.

The first time I saw the movie *The Bodyguard,* with Whitney Houston, I thought I was watching a documentary of my own life, with all the tensions and difficulties of putting on that kind of show. (I love Whitney, by the way, and think she was great in the film. Her husband, Bobby Brown, happens to be a distant relative of mine. Talk about a small world!)

One time in Venezuela we were onstage in a stadium playing to twenty-five thousand packed-in people. In South America they don't charge a lot of money for admission but make their profits in sponsorships, concessions, and refreshments. A lot of beer gets guzzled. During the show, people started getting rowdy and throwing cans and bottles up in the air. By the time I got to "Love to Love You Baby," the press of drunken people against the stage was so overwhelming it moved our stage fifty feet back, until we were pushed against the rear wall of the stadium! Chaos broke out as people started trampling one another. I was barely able to escape. One of our local bodyguards' daughters was caught in the melee and wound up with a broken arm.

It was out of control and so scary, especially since my daughter and my younger sister were with me that day.

On one of our South American stops I was being interviewed by a reporter from UPI who couldn't stop looking at me in a very strange way. When I finally asked him what the matter was, he said, "Oh, nothing. Except, you know, you really don't look at all like a man."

"A man . . . me?" I said. "I have a daughter. I'm the real thing. What man can do that?" I smiled sweetly and said, "I'm no man, baby."

I realized that the rumor had made its way south. I was just going to have to learn to live with it. That was the first time I realized how painful a lie could be. Success has its price.

✳

Once you become a public figure, your life is no longer . . . *your life*. It belongs to somebody else. To *everybody* else! There is an energy that comes into play that has nothing to do with who you are.

My adventures in Germany had had an element of rebellion to them, but even that rebellion did not prepare me for what followed in the wake of "Love to Love You Baby." I had no idea how to handle the success, or where to turn for help. Part of the problem was that Neil had created a completely new persona for me, which had absolutely nothing to do with who I really was. During my acting career in Munich, for instance, I had always been the comedic one in our group, a clown, Lucille Ball–like. In fact, they used to refer to me as "Little Lucy."

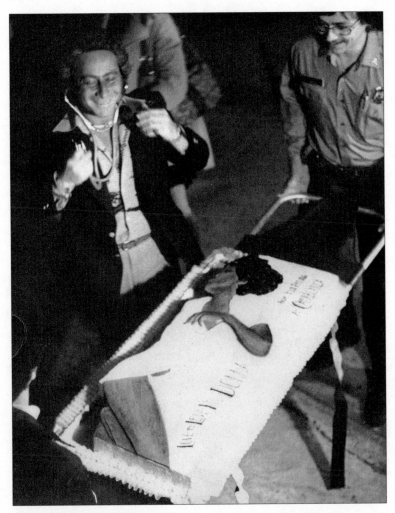

Buck Reingold from Casablanca Records ushering the infamous *Love to Love You Baby* cake into an ambulance.

Photo courtesy of the Sudano family archives

While the overtly sexual content of "Love to Love You Baby" was a problem for me, the relentless hype by the label to cast me as a real-life sex goddess drove me crazy. Even a *Time* magazine article described me as the Queen of Sex-Rock, which I found appalling. As far as I was concerned, singing "Love to Love You Baby" was just an acting exercise, a mere performance of me trying to imagine what the song would sound like if Marilyn Monroe were singing it. My normal singing voice has never sounded anything like the voice I made up for that song, before or since.

Compared to what young performers are doing today, "Love to Love You Baby" wasn't all that far out, but at its time it was groundbreaking. It was initially banned in England and on several stations in America. Women in show business back then didn't act or sing "that way" even if they *were* "that way." What was unique about "Love to Love You Baby" was that it created a powerful, feminine image that was unlike anything previously released in pop music. It was an image I regretted. I mean, who could live up to that? Not even Marilyn!

Because of my strong religious faith, I felt very guilty about allowing myself to publicly be made into a false and prurient sex goddess. This was not a direction or image I was comfortable with. I felt that the sensuality minimalized my self-worth and made people think that I had prostituted my talent to advance my career. Don't get me wrong: sex is a beautiful thing in the right context, and I'm not a prude. But flaunting myself in this manner went totally against my moral grain.

On the stage back in Germany, I'd felt protected by the distance between me and the audience. Now, in America, I was trapped under the scrutiny of the television lens, and the TV brought out every insecurity I'd ever had, from my facial scar to my skinny arms. I began to worry all over again about how others saw me. I asked cameramen not to photograph me from my so-called bad side, where the scar was. This made people think I was some kind of prima donna, when actually just the opposite was true. I was insecure about my ordinariness. I felt unqualified for being fussed over and totally unsuited for the part.

I felt completely ill at ease with all the promotion, attention, and responsibilities necessary to keep the record selling. At Neil's personal directive, I always wore sensuous costumes. I was choreographed so that my outstretched arms would do a sort of wave motion and I would manipulate the microphone in a very suggestive fashion while smoke was blown between my legs. At one point, in a show, I actually emerged from a gigantic egg in pure Spinal Tap fashion.

I had four male dancers wearing loincloths. One day one of them forgot to put his loincloth on. He went onstage clad only in his jockstrap. The audience thought it was part of the show and went wild! I looked down and all I could see was his cute brown gluteus maximus staring back at me! Can you imagine having to sing "Love to Love You Baby" with that kind of show in front of your father, who happened to be in the audience that night? I did, and I have never heard the end of it!

The audiences' reactions never failed to amaze me. They'd rip their clothes off, run down the aisles, and throw their garments onto the stage! Men's and women's underwear and even bras would be thrown at my feet. I'd had no idea my music was going to make people do *that*! It quickly got to the point where the music would start and once a first few recognizable bars were played, the audience would become completely uncontrollable!

Whenever I went out on the road, I'd have an entourage of no less than thirty-five people with me, including dancers, musicians, crew, bodyguards, and a conductor for the orchestra. The touring was becoming very expensive.

Now, coming from a theatrical background, I knew how costly staging a show could become. While sitting in Neil's office one day, I said to him, alluding to the excessive spending, "Neil, I want to be rich." He said, "No, Donna, you want to live like you're rich." I said, "No, I want to *be* rich! Rich! Rich!" I wanted to make a profit while still putting on the absolute best show I could.

✳

During this time I felt my life slipping more out of my control. I couldn't even wear my own street clothes during the day. Neil insisted that I had to always "play" Donna the Sex Symbol, because it was part of my job to make the audience believe that's who I really was. I had to suffer through an endless litany of *walk this way, talk this way, wear your hair this way, say this, do this, don't say this, don't say that.* I hated the relentless focus on my outward appearance, though I'm sure it was necessary at the time. But what about the other me—didn't she get to say something about it?

I had also been instructed by Neil that no matter what I was doing I always had to be polite and sign autographs, that it was all "part of the business of being famous." I began to comprehend that the business of show business is the industrialization of talent. The art of fame is as difficult to practice as the art of singing, painting, or acting. The most difficult thing for me during this time was to remain my own person within the machine, to hold on to my real identity, to the me nobody knows.

As my success continued I received two additional gold records, one for *A Love Trilogy* and one for the *Four Seasons of Love* album, which, by the way, gave me the opportunity to replicate a number of very recognizable movie poses. I even dared, as a black woman, to portray the famous *Seven Year Itch* Marilyn Monroe pose, which continued to perpetuate my sexual image, to Neil's delight.

As a result, the more successful I became, the more of an impasse I faced whenever I saw myself. But the louder the music got, the more difficult it became for me to hear the answer. I began to dislike the me I was becoming.

In 1976, we expanded our show to include concert venues, and I opened for many of the biggest acts of the day, including the Temptations and the Spinners. Although I grew up on and loved R&B music, I was much more of a pop-rock, folk-oriented artist. But my skin was brown, so I was automatically packaged as an R&B act. Neil assured me that this was all about to change as I transitioned from a supporting to a headlining act.

One of my first headlining performances would turn out to be an experience I'd rather forget. I was booked to perform at

My first gold record, circa 1975. Left to right: Cecil Holmes, Giorgio Moroder, me, and Neil Bogart. *Photo by Dagmar*

the famous Roseland dance hall in New York City, to an over-sold show. There were so many people crowded on the dance floor, it created an almost suffocating humidity. In addition, the press of flesh against the speakers caused my voice to sound muffled and distorted. The sound was positively awful. The next morning the *Daily News* printed a beautiful photo of me and a review of the show. I was so excited until I read the caption: "A rose that stinks." I could have laughed or cried. I paused for a moment, then laughed. The review was right! I didn't stink, but one couldn't tell because no one could actually hear the show.

✳

Headlining may have been great for my career, but it also meant I had to carry the whole show, which put even more of a strain on my health, both physically and mentally. Now worldwide, the tour had other, more far-reaching effects as well. Halfway through our European leg of the tour Helmuth showed up in Boston and tried to take Mimi away. Legally he had a pretty good case, as the laws in Austria favor the father. He had gotten himself a lawyer and was asking for permanent custody. I knew that if he got it, he would undoubtedly take Mimi back to Austria, and that meant I had to buy some time while I completed the necessary steps to get her full citizenship. I called Helmuth and spoke to him directly. I felt I knew at that time what he wanted and promised him we'd work it out. I thought that Mimi wasn't his goal, that what he really wanted was to reconcile, and that he was using our daughter as a way of pressuring me—a strategy that, I'm afraid, wouldn't work.

My separation from Mimi, Gunther's ongoing threats, and Helmuth's pressure made me feel that my independence was slowly being taken away. I had come to hate every minute of the tour, knowing that my obligation to my career had put my daughter's future in jeopardy. I was lost and felt suicidal. It happened one day toward the end of 1976. We were staying at the Navarro Hotel on Central Park South.

I had just returned to New York City from yet another burst of promotional dates, and I still felt a fair degree of disorientation from all my flying around the country. At times I became so disoriented I would lapse into German in the middle of a conversation. This made some people think I was being pretentious, which I wasn't. I was simply confused about where I was, what I was doing, and why. I was experiencing culture shock.

On top of that, because I didn't have a lot of friends in New York, I usually wound up spending most of my free time alone. Not that I ever had all that much free time. To make matters worse, Gunther and I had gotten back together shortly before we returned to America. In order to give Gunther something to do, Neil, who had immediately sized up the situation, arranged to have Gunther make his lithographs at the Circle Fine Arts atelier in lower Manhattan. Neil's idea was to keep Gunther occupied so he would leave me alone. Sure enough, Neil's tactic worked. Gunther had his ego stroked, and plunged himself into the preparations for his show, spending all his time at the gallery to make sure his work was displayed the way he wanted it to be.

Still, Gunther's manic jealousy did not let up. Just as he had in Germany, he once again tried to take control of my private life. I couldn't take it anymore. On one side I had Helmuth trying to take my daughter away from me. On the other side, I had Neil trying to keep me out on the road, and in the middle I had Gunther smothering me. Gunther wanted Neil to back off, Neil wanted Gunther to leave me alone, and Helmuth wanted me and Mimi back. It was a royal mess.

No matter how confused I was, I knew I no longer wanted to be controlled by another human being. I had to figure out some way to get out from under Gunther's possessiveness. His presence was a dark oppressive cloud that constantly hung over my head.

On this particular day, while Gunther was away at the Manhattan gallery, I was in bed watching TV. Not any particular program—just the TV itself. The set had gone on the blink the night before, and I found myself staring at the horizontal lines going up, up, up putting me into a hypnotic state. Suddenly I was overcome by an overwhelming sensation of profound despair and uselessness. I felt emotionally destitute, trapped with only one way out. I'd had similar feelings in the past, but these feelings were more intense than ever. I truly believed that no one in the world was *ever* going to know the real me. I felt like I was living a big fat lie. I had to get out. Somehow, I had to be free from this insanity.

The day was winter-short, and the eerie light faded fast and unforgiving. I had thoughts that kept repeating in my head, rolling like the TV screen, that I couldn't turn off. I had failed God. I was worthless. I couldn't be forgiven. I was doomed for hell.

Believing I was without God made me feel truly and completely alone and utterly desperate.

Those dark thoughts forced me out of bed. I walked over to the big, heavy hotel window, threw it open, and hoped the weight of my loneliness would send me crashing eleven stories to the sidewalk below.

As I put my right leg out and shifted my weight to the left, my foot somehow got caught as the drapes bunched around the curved radiator pipes. I was trying to shake the curtain off my leg when the door to the room swung open and in walked the maid. She looked at me for several seconds, startled. For the longest time, she stood frozen and said nothing.

I too was frozen, and I stayed that way, with my body halfway out the window, until finally she stammered, "Oh, Mrs. Summer, can I come in and clean your room now?" Flooded with shame, I was shocked back to reality.

A rush of panic shot through my whole body, jolting me back to my senses. I knew I was in a bad place in my head, which God knew as well. But He'd put those drapes there for me to get caught on, providing enough time for Him to send in the maid to save me from jumping. In that instant my head began to spin. I was humbled. What right did I have to take my life? I remembered how—so long ago, it seemed—God had told me I would one day become famous. He had kept His word. I knew I had been wrong to want to hurt myself, to betray the fulfillment of that promise. I needed to get medical help, real help.

As soon as I got hold of myself, I placed a call to Neil in

California. When he got on the phone I relayed to him what had just happened. He told me to hold on, that he'd take care of everything. He immediately called a friend of his, Dr. Edward Jannica, and made arrangements for me to see him at his Los Angeles office. Then Neil arranged for me to fly to L.A. that night. Less than twenty-four hours after trying to leap out that New York City window, I was in Dr. Jannica's office.

He sat and listened for a long time as I poured my heart out, trying to explain to him how and why I felt so bad. When I finally finished, he said he understood exactly what I was going through and he believed he could help me. He said he suspected that the problem was a chemical imbalance in my brain, that my serotonin levels were off and that most likely I needed something called an MAO inhibitor. This condition, he said, was particularly prevalent among creative people. He emphatically reassured me that I wasn't suffering from a "mental" problem at all, but rather a *physical* one; it was as simple and unprofound as a fluid imbalance in my brain. He told me that after all I'd been through, it was completely understandable that my imbalance had intensified. Any one of a number of my circumstances could have triggered my depression. The physical change of continents alone, followed by culture shock and the anxiety associated with a grueling tour, could easily have pushed the strongest person over the edge. It was a testament to my mental fortitude that I'd actually lived for so long with this condition undiagnosed.

That set me thinking. I had been taken away from all my friends and my home in Germany and transplanted back to the

U.S. I had been in an American cultural vacuum from 1968 to 1975 and was totally unprepared for my return to the States. I began to realize that people would say things to me and I'd have no idea what they were talking about. For example, one morning during the tour I was on an early-morning talk show with one of the top early-morning celebrities in the country and I had no idea who he was. I remembered how I'd panicked during a commercial break and how, sensing my panic, Susan Munao had run over and slipped me a piece of paper with his name on it. It was exactly that intense fear and anxiety that Dr. Jannica was talking about. Now, sitting in his office, I realized that even though I was becoming a celebrity in America, I felt as if I were coming out of solitary confinement. Basically, I was lost in time.

Dr. Jannica prescribed something called Marplan, an MAO inhibitor. As soon as I started taking it, I knew my foot had come off that ledge for good and would not go back. It took about two months for my body to completely acclimate to the proper dosage. Under Dr. Jannica's close supervision, I increased the dosage in stages until I reached the daily amount that was right for me. After that, I became more focused, more productive than I had been at any other time in my life.

In fact, too much so. After being someone who had to be coaxed out of bed, now I found I could easily go three or four days without sleeping. I sped through life, ignoring all the opposing traffic and illuminated stop signs. On the positive side, I resumed my tour, I performed live without fear on network TV, and I wrote great new songs and arrangements for my next album. On the negative side, I began to think faster than I could talk. I would start sentences and not finish them, which drove everyone around me crazy. And I'd go for days without having any desire to eat anything except chocolate.

Eventually, it became clear to me that the medicine I was taking had no shutoff valve, that I was firing on all cylinders all the time. It took me quite a while to recognize the sometimes subtle side effects, and how to compensate. For example, my diet was restricted to avoid severe reactions with my medication. It became a constant battle to keep my body in sync.

Nevertheless, it was worth it. My ability to cope with fear had, at last, been fortified synthetically.

As I began to function ever more normally, at least initially I was able to set new and more realistic goals for myself, although I didn't want to be on this or any medicine forever. I wanted to find a different kind of "normalizer," a regulator that worked without chemicals, something permanent.

And I knew the way to find it: it was time to get in touch with my inner self. I had to rediscover the strength inherent in my spirit and soul. I had to find God and hear from Him personally.

9

Thank God It's Friday

My world tour finally ended early in 1977, after which I returned, exhausted but exhilarated, to a small but lovely house on five acres at 2720 Benedict Canyon, with a great front lawn for Mimi to eventually run and roll around on.

I have to say that Neil was ecstatic over my success, and with good reason. I was the first performer on Casablanca who came out of the chute and went directly to the top. More often than not, the head honcho of a record label is either some ex-hippie and entertainer who loves music but knows nothing about business, or a businessman who doesn't care about the music. Neil was one of those rare people in our industry who loved both sides—the music *and* the business.

For the longest time I felt blessed that Neil had chosen to deal with me on an artistic level first and on a business level second. Together with Giorgio and Pete Bellotte, we were instrumental in changing the sound and direction of popular music.

Listen to Blondie's "Heart of Glass" or Madonna's "Borderline" and see if you don't hear echoes of Giorgio's techno influence. Reportedly, when John Lennon first heard one of our early hits, "I Feel Love," he locked himself in a room and listened to it over and over again, saying, "This is the future."

The motif of the Casablanca Records offices on Sunset Boulevard was based on the famous Bogart film of the same name. (Neil's real last name was Bogatz, which he'd changed in homage to his hero.) From the design of the label's logo, to the offices of the publishing company, Rick's Music, to the entire decor of the building, everything was made to look as if it were from a film-fantasy version of Casablanca. Going to Neil's office was like a pilgrimage to a Hollywood back lot. It was actually a lot of fun. Indeed, Neil's endless zest for life appealed to me. It helped me learn how to enjoy this new phase of my life.

And speaking of Hollywood back lots, Casablanca Records began to expand into the movie business. Neil and his new partner, Peter Guber, had arranged for me to work with John Barry, one of Hollywood's great music composers. Wow, an inexperienced girl like me in such elite company as the Oscar winner John Barry, being asked to cowrite the theme for the movie *The Deep*.

I was now living in my house on Benedict Canyon, an elegant three-bedroom ranch decked out in Hollywood style, with a big master suite, an L-shaped couch, and an Olympic-sized swimming pool. Tinseltown, oddly enough, was growing on me.

L.A. was liberating and lively. It also has the greatest weather imaginable, especially for someone who was used to

With my niece at the piano. *Photo courtesy of the Sudano family archives*

German winters. Fresh from the hip European musical and theatrical scene, I now found myself on the other side of the pop cultural world. I had become the so-called Queen of Disco, hob-nobbing with many of the legends of rock 'n' roll and partying on Sunset Boulevard.

Sunset Boulevard was a lively, full-spectrum street. Beautiful women and handsome men were everywhere. The high-end dress shops and the low-end leather lounges, the fancy restaurants and outdoor cafés, the all-night clubs and the early-morning newsstands all helped give the street a rhythm as catchy as anything I'd ever laid down on a record.

One of the great joys for me was hanging out at the great industry-favored restaurants. Although I liked trying new foods, I was always a fussy eater. In L.A. it was possible for me to find a place that was open and catered to my particular likes day or night. Sometimes the eateries would provide a private room. If not, people would more often than not respect my privacy.

Whenever I was in the mood for solid American food, I would go to the Polo Lounge at the Beverly Hills Hotel on Sunset Boulevard, or the Palm Restaurant on Santa Monica Boulevard, down the hill from Casablanca's offices. Bernice and George Altschul, the mommy and daddy of disco, were king and queen of Carlos and Charlie's, a fun faux-Mexican food place that had one of the swingingest clubs in all of L.A. And then, of course, there was Mr. Chow's in Beverly Hills whenever I was in the mood for Chinese.

The Château Marmot was then, and still is, a favorite hotel of the Hollywood in-crowd, nestled on a hill behind my favorite

Beverly Hills shops. The hotel lobby was *the* place to meet someone. There was also the Brown Derby, Joe Allen's, and the legendary Martoni's, on Cahuenga, just south of Sunset. A victim of the 1994 earthquake, Martoni's is now gone, but it will always be remembered by anyone who ever ate their extraordinary shrimp. I practically lived in the back room at Martoni's. I became friendly with the owner, Sal Martoni, and whenever I didn't feel like cooking at home, Sal would send over all the food I could ever want right to my front door.

Of course there was El Compadre on Sunset, a wonderful family-oriented Mexican restaurant everyone in the music biz favored. It's been there forever, complete with the same mariachi band that plays terrific live music all through the night. Greenblatt's and Nate 'n' Al's in Beverly Hills were the best Jewish delis in town and served up the most amazing chicken soup. Greenblatt's was directly across from Schwab's drugstore, where a copy of the then-hard-to-find daily *New York Times* was always available for us regulars to read. For a more "detailed" breakfast, Duke's was the only place to go. It was part of the infamous Tropicana Hotel, the requisite hangout for every self-respecting rock group in town.

The atmosphere at Duke's was as strong as its coffee, a cup of which could strip the paint off your car. The same atmosphere, the same people, and, for all intents and purposes, the same food was available at Barney's Beanery, the place to hang when the sun went down and until it came up again (at which time it was back to Duke's for breakfast).

However, my all-time favorite haunt was Roy's, hands

down the most unique Chinese restaurant that ever existed! It was tucked a half block south of the Sunset Strip, and everyone who was anyone in the music business sooner or later congregated at Roy's. It was owned and operated by Roy Silver and backed financially by, among others, Neil Bogart. The decor of the place was more like a dimly lit recording studio than the standard imitation Chinese. It was laid out in four distinct sections: the bar; the main room; the private booths, which came complete with curtains; and, for the very few, the "private room."

After gaily greeting us at the door, Frances, the hostess with long dancer legs, would usher us into the bar for a drink. We would frequently find ourselves two to three bodies deep in the standing-room-only bar. Crazy as it seems, it always felt like home. It was so comfortable no one wanted to leave. Ultimately closing time would arrive, and then they would literally ask us to go home.

I was always amazed by the personable conversations with strangers that occurred there with ease. The famous would mingle and mesh with the everyday patrons like old friends, and all social classes seemed to melt away. At Roy's *everyone* was special. "Industry" was the common language, and we all spoke it.

There were enormous tables with tiny lights around the edges, and the menus were printed on giant playing cards. You shuffled through the "deck" and handed your waitress the "cards" with the dishes you wanted. Roy prepared Chinese food in a most delightful and unusual way. He had the best chicken wings in the world. The rice, the little ribs, the shrimp—all of it was so mag-

nificent! The food tasted like nothing you'd ever eaten anywhere! Even the desserts were special, featuring such novel
items as frozen Milky Ways with little fortunes embedded in
them. Yes, Roy's was *the* place in those days, the closest thing to
the music industry's version of the legendary Brown Derby, the
restaurant that, at one time, was the social center in the world of
film.

I have so many amazing memories of Roy's, including hanging with many Hollywood celebrities. David Janssen, TV's dash-
ing, dark, and romantic "fugitive" was often there at the bar.
(Hmmmmm, if Lieutenant Gerard only knew!) Sammy Davis
Jr., another celebrity regular, would love to tease me. Every time
he'd see me he'd say, "Come on, Donna, who did your nose?" I
would laugh hysterically. "If I could choose my nose," I'd say, "do
you think I would choose this one? Sammy," I'd say, "you want to
see pictures of me as a child? *This is my real nose!*"

"Sweetheart," he'd say, "*nobody* has a nose like that."

If I saw him first, I would burst into a comic-operatic version of "The Candy Man." He was such a good-natured soul. I
loved him, I absolutely loved him.

One night, the horror king himself, Vincent Price, was sitting in the booth next to mine. At one point I got up to go to the
ladies' room. I was wearing a long, very pretty sweater, complete with leggings and boots, a very Munich look, to be sure.
When I came back, Vincent stood up and said, "I've got to look
at you!" It struck me as the funniest thing, because he was so
charming and debonair, nothing like those creepy lunatics he
played in the movies. "I just wanted to admire your sweater," he

said, smiling in his scary, charming way. His wife gave me a glance as if to say, It's not the sweater, honey, it's what's inside. Her expression was so funny we all fell out laughing.

*

I was in the midst of recording the *I Remember Yesterday* album when Joyce Bogart, now Neil's wife, decided to take me for a driving lesson one afternoon. If I lived in L.A., she kept telling me, I had to know how to drive. And where I was living, there was no other way to come and go except by car.

So there we were driving around L.A. with Joyce trying to teach me how to use a stick shift. After several jerky stops and starts, I pulled over to take a break in front of Susan Munao's building. Susan came out and asked us if we wanted to come up and meet three friends from her neighborhood in Brooklyn, whom she'd helped get signed to Millennium Records.

I decided to end the driving-lesson torture for the day, said good-bye to an exhausted Joyce, and went inside. The group was three young men, Joe Esposito, Eddie Hokenson, and Bruce Sudano, who called themselves Brooklyn Dreams. They had given up their old L.A. apartment under the belief that they were headed to New York to record their first album. When their plans had changed abruptly and they'd suddenly found themselves homeless, Susan had come to the rescue. As a result, they were living out of boxes in a couple of rooms in her apartment while trying to find apartments in Irvine, about an hour outside of L.A. It was at Susan's place that I first laid eyes on Bruce Sudano.

Here I am backstage with Joyce Bogart (left) and Susan Munao.
Photographer unknown; photo courtesy of the Sudano family archives

My reaction to him was immediate and visceral, and somehow I knew that he felt the same way about me. It was as if I could hear his innermost thoughts out loud! I had never felt like that with any other man. I knew instantly in my heart that I was going to marry this man one day. But that wouldn't be easy.

Despite all the love electricity in the air that afternoon, Bruce remained cool, way cool. I was in the midst of a tremendous amount of success, while he was still on the verge of obtaining his dreams. The other two guys, Joe and Eddie, were loose and easy with me, but Bruce left, saying he had somewhere else to go. Okay, I said to myself, go and do your thing; but if you come back, you are going to be *miiiiiiine*!

He returned in forty-five minutes. Yep, I knew it.

Of course, at the time a new romantic involvement was just about the last thing I was looking for. I'd already "done the marriage thing" and was still negotiating with Helmuth for custody of Mimi. And I had Gunther to contend with; he was about to leave New York City and come to live with me full-time at the Benedict Canyon house. Nevertheless, I began hanging out with Bruce, Joe, and Eddie. The more I got to know Bruce, the more he became my safe and sane haven from all of Gunther's craziness. From the beginning I respected Bruce as a musician, as a writer, and as a man, but I was too frightened of the long reach of Gunther's tyrannical clutches to become physically involved.

One thing I shared with Bruce was music. When I found out he was a composer, I wanted to write some songs with him. Ever since "Love to Love You Baby," I'd wanted to do some more writing, but I felt inadequate because I couldn't read music or play an instrument. With Giorgio I'd only written lyrics, or come up with catchphrases like "Love to love you baby." I had learned form and structure from Giorgio, but with Bruce I had finally met someone who could teach me how to put music to my words—how to use all my senses, how to visualize a song, and how to say what I saw in a very real way.

Bruce had gotten his songwriting training in New York City, under the hard thumb of the notorious Morris Levy. Like so many other aspiring songwriters, Bruce worked like a dog and never saw a royalty statement. He cowrote a Top Ten hit, "Ball of Fire," with Tommy James, and his former band, Alive n' Kickin', had had a number three song, "Tighter, Tighter."

I also discovered that Bruce had a special talent for transforming descriptive scenes from the street into emotionally fulfilling music that appealed to me. We used to get together for songwriting sessions early in the morning, and spend all day and all night writing and singing songs till the sun came up the next day. When I was in town, of course.

I felt connected to Bruce's music. His songs spoke directly to me, and I sensed early on that I could learn a lot from him, and that perhaps there was something he could learn from me, too. The fact that he was extremely handsome and I was incredibly attracted to him didn't exactly act as a deterrent! Bruce, however, had a total disregard for his exceptional good looks. He had a calm and cool kind of cockiness, which I attributed to his Italianness. Man, was he sexy!

In those days I wore a lot of wigs, although my own hair

Left to right: Joe Esposito of the Brooklyn Dreams, Don Wasley of Casablanca Records, Susan Munao, Bruce Sudano, Bruce Bird of Casablanca Records, and Eddie Hokenson of the Brooklyn Dreams.

Photo by Judi Lesta

was about shoulder length. One morning when I went to pick up Bruce, I walked into the house without my usual prefab do. "Well, guys, this is the real me!" I said, pointing to my head. "Either you like it or you don't." The others kidded me, but I wanted Bruce to see me the way I truly was, maybe for no other reason than to test his early feelings for me. I didn't want to wear any masks, and I didn't want any makeup to cover my emotional scars. Whenever I was alone with the Brooklyn Dreams, I went "au naturel." With them I could be the real me, and I loved that freedom.

Around this time we had our first opportunity to collaborate together. The Brooklyn Dreams sang background vocals on the *I Remember Yesterday* album. Then the guys moved to Irvine, California, to record their debut album. This became the impetus for me to finally get my driver's license, so I could see them when I was in town. I returned the collaboration favor and sang with them on Bruce's song "Old Fashioned Girl."

Even though there was nothing physical between us, whenever I left L.A. I couldn't get Bruce out of my mind. I began to keep a secret diary, filling its pages with how much I missed Bruce.

✳

Because my initial feelings for Bruce were so strong, I could hardly stand to be around him without wanting to . . . *be with him*. But I had Gunther to deal with. In 1977, Gunther decided it was time he came out to Los Angeles.

Bruce was resolute in not wanting to make a full-time commitment to me. For one thing, he didn't think mixing work with pleasure was a good idea. For another, he already had a steady girlfriend and he knew I was still involved with Gunther, and he wasn't the kind of guy to get between another man and his woman. His honor was driving me crazy, but I appreciated it, although all the while Gunther's madness was posing a threat to my life.

✳

Ever since he'd arrived in L.A., Gunther had been uneasy about Bruce. My insistence that there was nothing physical between us only made him even more jealous, to the point of insanity. I would come home and Gunther would be waiting to confront me, accusing me of having an affair with Bruce. He was right, at least in terms of my desire.

One afternoon, I came home and Gunther demanded to know where I had been. "I was out with the boys," I replied. "The boys," he said. "What boys?" I was standing in the garage, walking toward the kitchen door, and Gunther followed me. Before I could say anything, he grabbed me, threw me up against the wall, and proceeded to slap me around. He bodily threw me across the garage. I banged on the door and yelled for someone to please help me. My personal assistant, Pat Naderhoff, was there, but she was on the other side of the house at first and couldn't hear me.

I was taking the brunt of Gunther's rage. He kept beating me when Pat finally heard my screams and opened the door. Gunther lunged after her, but she managed to escape to another part of the house and hid. He then turned back to me, grabbed my arm, and threw me into the laundry room, where he continued to beat me up. I fell into a heap, and Gunther disappeared. After a moment he returned, with a gun in his hands. Was he going to kill me? He waved the gun and started toward me. He was staring with that insane madman look that scared me to my core.

At that point, the phone began to ring, sounding as loud and as insistent as a fire alarm. Finally, Gunther picked it up; it was Susan Munao, calling me from New York. When Gunther, who was out of breath, said I couldn't come to the phone, Susan knew immediately that something was seriously wrong. She demanded that he put me on. Instead, he kept talking to her, stating how wrong I was and that he was not a fool. Susan was convinced that something was wrong. While keeping him on the line, she had her assistant call Neil at his office and tell him to get the police to my house immediately.

Before Gunther could hang up the phone, the LAPD had surrounded the place. Neil was with them. They broke into the house and arrested Gunther. I was still alive and knew, amidst the shattered pieces of glass and debris, that I had to find the strength to start over. "I must begin again," I told myself. Battered, bruised, and beaten nearly to death, I realized that God had come to my rescue yet again.

Neil insisted I stay at his guest house for the next few days, and he hired a phalanx of security guards to protect me.

Within days Gunther was booked for assault and battery, had his visa revoked, and was expelled from the country.

I was relieved and also frightened when I got word of Gunther's deportation. I was finally free from his maniacal grip, yet terrified to be alone.

*

By this time, I'd managed to negotiate a settlement with Helmuth, and Mimi came out to the West Coast to live with me. And thank God my youngest sister, Dara, who was already one of the backup singers in my show, was there to help me look after Mimi. After a frightening incident with a nanny, I was wary of having anybody but my family help me take care of my daughter.

Mimi had always been an extremely healthy, vibrant child. As a baby and to this day she's always had the disposition of an angel. However, one time when I came back unexpectedly from a road trip, I was shocked to discover how lethargic Mimi had become. Her once-bright blue eyes were half-closed. I asked the nanny if she knew what was wrong with Mimi. "Oh no," she said. "Nothing's wrong with the little girl. That is how she always looks when she wakes up." My maternal instinct kicked in.

Besides, I knew Mimi always woke up bright-eyed, happy, and singing. I began to wonder just who this nanny was and what she was doing when she was alone with my baby. I kept my cool and gave her a weekend off. As soon as she left the house I went to her room, searched it, and found a suspicious medicine hidden in her dresser drawer. The bottle contained strong medicine to calm hyperactive children! She was drugging my child so she wouldn't have to deal with her! It was as if

Left to right: Bruce, Susan Munao, and I. *Photo courtesy of Susan Munao*

some nightmarish scene from a B horror movie had played out in my very own home.

And that wasn't all. She'd have her entire family over to the house whenever I was gone. I discovered this after I found strange toys scattered around the house. I asked a few of my neighbors if they'd noticed anything unusual when I wasn't around. They told me, yes, there were lots of strange people in the house and several children they didn't recognize on the front lawn whenever I traveled.

I was enraged! When the nanny returned, I told her to pack her things and get out, and that if I ever saw her face again I would immediately call the police and have her arrested for attempting to kill my daughter. I never saw or heard from her again.

With the trauma of my daughter still fresh in my mind and my overall exhaustion from a year and a half of nonstop performing, I began to feel the wear and tear of being on the road, and my body clock was completely off. Ultimately, I was so grateful to have my own family taking care of Mimi.

I truly loved Neil and was grateful for all that he had done and was doing for me, but I also felt the short leash he kept me on was becoming too tight. For instance, making his wife one of my managers seemed to me a major conflict of interest, and I wasn't the only one who felt it. Giorgio would take me aside and in his gentle fashion urge me to drop Joyce, saying it was impossible for her to manage me objectively at the same time she was married to the head of my record company. Foolishly, I resisted his wise advice. Joyce was a friend, and I believed that

Neil was doing everything in the world for my career. However, Giorgio was, well, Giorgio, and like a big brother to me. I felt I could trust him. I listened to what he said, thought there was some merit to his concern, but had no idea what to do about it. Then finally the bulb went off in my head, and I got it. I was so new to all of this, not only didn't I have a lawyer, I didn't even know I needed one, at least not yet.

✳

Nineteen seventy-seven was an unpredictable year. While waiting—hoping is probably more accurate—for Bruce to become disentangled from his girlfriend, I started dating a musician by the name of Michael. He was a good-looking, blond-haired, blue-eyed surfer boy. I liked him well enough, but I made it clear to him from the start that I would leave him if Bruce ever became available.

Around this time I had the opportunity to appear in a motion picture. *Thank God It's Friday* was dreamed up by Paul Jabara and Neil to take further advantage of their corner on the disco craze.

Paul was a very animated New Yorker with a Lebanese background. He had been an actor in movies and theater from the time he was a young boy. He loved show business. We'd met back in the *Hair* days and had become good friends. Paul had first heard me belting out songs on the stage in Europe. When my first records were released, he wasn't satisfied with all my breathy cooing. He wanted me to sing out loud, in full voice. He trapped me in the bathroom in a hotel in Puerto Rico and sang

"Last Dance" to me over and over again until I consented to do it. Thank God he did.

I had a small acting part in the film, but it was my singing of "Last Dance" that became the movie's major selling point, and gave me one of the biggest hits of my career.

Jeff Goldblum, a young actor whose career was about to explode, was the star of the film. He was soon to be at the top of Hollywood's newest crop of leading men, and his talent was matched by that of his costars, Debra Winger and Valerie Landsburg, later of the television version of *Fame*. Jeff and I became friends during the shooting of *Thank God It's Friday*. He was such a mischief maker with a great sense of humor. He walked around the set all day acting like a combination of the real Nutty Professor and a genuine brainiac and kept me in stitches the whole time.

For me, 1978 was an amazing year. I won my first Grammy, for Best Female R&B Vocal Performance, for "Last Dance." I won another Grammy for my version of the Jimmy Webb classic "MacArthur Park." "Last Dance" also won a Golden Globe and was nominated for the Academy Award that year for Best Song. If that wasn't enough, I received an invitation to perform "Last Dance" at the Academy Awards ceremony in spring of 1979. I was elated!

On the morning of the awards we flew in a private jet from Las Vegas to Los Angeles to rehearse and do the show live at the Dorothy Chandler Pavillion. I can't tell you how impressive it was to meet and converse casually with some of the biggest names in Hollywood: Gregory Peck, Charlton Heston, and Dean Martin, to name a few. I was backstage, sitting at the bar in the greenroom with Susan Munao, Paul Jabara, and James Coburn (along with his unmistakable smile), as the announcers approached the category in which "Last Dance" was nominated. I felt such an immense excitement build up within me, to the point where I could not hold back any longer . . . I let out a bloodcurdling scream just seconds before the winner of the Oscar for that year's Best Song was announced: "Last Dance." They called out the song and I just continued to scream. I went out onstage with Paul to accept the award.

We immediately headed back to Las Vegas just in time to do an evening show, where I was able to share my exciting experience with the audience. What a thrill! Soon after, my agent from the William Morris Agency, Marty Beck, a suave, good-looking man-about-town sometimes known in the inner circle as Chickie-Baby, negotiated a long-term contract for me to headline at the MGM Grand Hotel. He'd been with us through the thick and thin of it and had been a part of every tour, every engagement, and nearly every deal for performing that I made.

In spite of all the accolades for "Last Dance," filming *Thank God It's Friday* was a disappointing experience for me. After all the years I'd spent in Europe developing my acting skills, I'd thought I would at last have a part in a film that would show off my ability and propel me on the path toward fulfilling my early dreams of becoming a movie actress. Instead I got cast in a ditsy role as a shy little girl who only wants a chance to sing, a kind of joke that runs throughout the film until I finally get to perform "Last Dance" at the end. In truth, there was virtually no acting required of me. After that experience, I knew the only types of roles I was going to be offered would be the *Fun in Acapulco* variety. I decided to give up any further attempts at a movie career. Hollywood saw me as a singer, and I was never going to shake that image by doing films like *Thank God It's Friday*.

So I returned to the thing I did best, making music, and did it with a vengeance.

10

Toot-Toot,
Beep-Beep

The 1978 world tour included Mexico, South America, and Europe, where my music continued to sell incredibly well. Everywhere I went, people would walk up to me and put things in my hand they wanted me to have, be it a coin, a picture of their baby, or a piece of clothing. Sometimes people would come up to me and say, "My mother was sick and she got healed listening to your music, and I want to give you something back."

Meanwhile, back in Boston, my mother would get fan mail for me from all over the world, some of which contained similar stories and mementos people wanted me to have. One time I called my mother from Europe and she told me how amazed she was at all the little gifts people would include with their letters. Then she said, "You know, Donna, I think you have a healing gift. There's healing in your voice."

Some of the stories my mother related to me were a bit overwhelming, and I was moved a great deal by them. One concerned a young boy who played "I Feel Love" on his record player at maximum volume while his deaf mother was vacuuming. Up until that time his mother had shown no signs of being able to hear any sound at all. Suddenly he noticed she was vacuuming in rhythm to the song, and mouthing the words! Then she burst out singing! Miraculously, she could hear. He told this story in a long letter and included with it a bunch of religious pins he wanted me to have.

Another time there was a girl who was a fan of mine and had been in a terrible car crash and was in a coma for days. When everything else failed, and the doctors had given up all hope, her parents started playing one of my albums continuously in the hospital room. One day not long after, she opened her eyes and recovered completely. These stories reinforced my belief that there is a lot more to music than we realize.

My mother was so excited about all the unusual letters and wanted to be more involved somehow. So when the tour ended, I eventually convinced my parents to settle in L.A. After so many years of being apart, I thought it would be nice for them to be closer to Mimi, my sister Dara, and me. Finally, after one especially heavy Boston snowstorm, she and Daddy both agreed.

I found it very helpful having my parents close by. Daddy had long been concerned about my safety, as had Neil, who made me very aware that I was no longer a private person anymore and needed to be very careful. Indeed, I was being stalked.

My stalker, Mr. X (as I'll call him), was a young actor whom I had worked with in the past. He would drop by my house when I wasn't home, bring gifts, and then ingratiate himself to my butler, Wilbert. I'd leave the house alone and spot him following me for blocks at a time. And then it got worse.

Once, in New York, I got a call from the front desk of the hotel telling me Mr. X was waiting for me in the lobby. I couldn't take it any longer, so I went down to the lobby with my bodyguards and asked him why he was following me. "You belong to me, Donna. We are supposed to be together. I *know* it," he said. That is when I really got scared. The next night after I had finished my performance, I spotted Mr. X standing by the backstage door with a smirky kind of smile on his face. I later discovered he had become friendly with some of my family members and coworkers, who had no idea he was stalking me.

I performed the next few months on the road, which temporarily took my mind off Mr. X.

By now Bruce had broken up with his girlfriend, and things had begun to cool between Michael and me. I decided the time had come to set all of this Bruce stuff straight, to confront in all honesty the man I truly desired.

Upon my return from the road, I'd left Michael, my on-again, off-again boyfriend, at home on Benedict Canyon and made a beeline over the hill to Bruce, who was renting an apartment off Santa Monica Boulevard. It was a temporary place, dreary the way furnished apartments can be, but home for him until he could find something better. He was surprised to see me standing in the doorway. We just stood there staring at each other silently, after months of waiting.

What is it about this guy, anyway? I thought to myself.

Have I met my match? Granted, he was very, very handsome, but that wasn't all of it. My heart was racing; I told it to calm down: *Just calm down. Not now, not now.* I had to maintain my cool. I had to appear a little aloof. After all, I had been away for a while and didn't know what had gone on in my absence. Was there someone else in the picture? I was like a leopardess softly stalking, eyeballing her prey. I'd always known that if I could find the door to this man, I could jimmy the lock, break in, and capture the hidden treasures. I stepped over the threshold without a word, still staring at him.

If he knew he could have had me without even "Hello," I'd lose his interest. The trick was to be around, but not around *too much;* to go out with other guys to keep Bruce constantly aware of my "market value," to keep my precious balance while continuing to work toward the ultimate goal. I had to capture his heart and undermine any preconceived notions. I had to fill up all his senses and intoxicate his masculinity with my femininity. I could tell he was playing the holding-back game. He's so good at playing it cool, I thought. He nonchalantly offered to let me spend the night. Oh, how my whole being screamed, *Yes, yes.* I wanted him so much I was tempted to break my own code. So, so tempted. I could feel his breath on my neck even though he was still standing across the room. I felt hot. Was the Diva of Love herself getting the vapors? Oh my!

I had to get out of there fast, before it was too late. I walked to the door, opened it, and ran to my car without the usual safety precautions of checking the street. By now it was night and the street was dark, really dark. I'd made it mindlessly all the way down Santa Monica Boulevard, up Doheny to Sunset Boulevard, then to Benedict Canyon when, out of nowhere, I saw a car behind me trying to pass.

I was right in the most dangerous curve in the road with no place to pull over. There had been so much oncoming traffic that someone would have to be a fool to try to pass at that precise place. The man in the car was forced to back off and get behind me. Again and again he tried to pass. I could almost see him. He was screaming at me and waving his arms like a lunatic.

I didn't know where to get off. What can I do? I thought. What can I do? Anxious, I raced like a woman possessed until I saw my house. With my blinker flashing, I quickly pulled into my driveway, and to my horror the man in the car defiantly pulled up behind me. I could feel him pull his car right up beside mine, jump out, and start toward me. It was so dark. I tried to scream for help, but nothing came out. I was terrified. What if this crazy man had a gun? I slammed my head against the steering wheel and covered my face with my arms and hands. The man banged against my car window, then opened my door.

I honked the horn, hoping Michael, who was in the house, would hear me. I felt the car door opening wider. I started screaming. I heard the voice of that man coming at me in the dark, belligerently screaming, "Get your clothes, you're coming home with me." I turned to look and gasped, to my surprise, to find Bruce standing over me, banging his hands against the roof of my car, crazed by what had just happened at his place and completely exasperated. Bruce had raced after me and chased me up Santa Monica, up Sunset, and all the way to Benedict Canyon to my door. Scarlett O'Hara, eat your heart out.

I sat there for a few minutes, amazed at the implications of this provocative act. Michael, who had come outside in the midst of the confusion, sensed that he was out of place and, scratching his blond surfer head, turned and went back into the house. Bruce leaned over and helped me out of the car. Out of nowhere the moon poked its half-lit face from behind a cloud and I thought to myself, This is no ordinary love song.

*

There was never any question that Bruce and I were going to wind up together no matter how many people there were between us. Now there were no other lovers and we were free to fall all the way in love. It didn't take long before he was spending more time with me than at his own apartment. By the end of the year we'd moved into a house together in the Hollywood Hills. It was a fabulous time of coming together for us, even if there was still one major rival Bruce had to fight for my attention: my career.

Neil had further increased his hold on the reins of my career. He'd stepped up his already considerable involvement in my public persona, continuing the periodic makeovers that completely recast my public look. He even went so far as to hire a French makeup specialist to ensure that I'd look exactly the way he wanted me to look whenever I went out. If I was about to go onstage and something was not right about my toenail polish, Neil would not think twice about getting down on his knees and fixing it himself. These simple things made me really love him.

Ironically, all his attention did nothing for my sense of self. I began to wonder if he was ever going to be satisfied with my appearance. The only place I found any real comfort was with Bruce, and even that was something of which Neil didn't approve. Having dispatched Gunther, Neil did not want to deal with yet another outside influence. The truth was, he wanted to sequester me as much as possible, believing that a lack of visibility enhanced my public mystique.

As a result, I had to be in touch with the office every day, and Neil personally had the contractual right of approval over anything I wanted to do professionally, including my occasional work with Bruce's group, the Brooklyn Dreams. My own office was in Neil's building, on Sunset, right on the first floor with Joyce, his wife. As Neil never failed to remind me, this was quite a privilege, as no other artist on the label was allowed to have space in that building.

If anybody, whether a reporter, another artist, or a co-worker, tried to get near me in any way while I was at the office, his private security would be all over them in a heartbeat. All of this kept twisting and turning me. On the one hand I was grateful for the protection and the concern, and on the other I felt he didn't trust me to look out for myself.

Because of Neil's Svengali-like role, I had almost no life outside the tiny space in which I ate, slept, and socialized with Bruce when I could get away. Looking back, it's no surprise to me that one of the songs I sang was called "Sunset People." It was not just about the people on the strip but the people who populated what my entire world had somehow become—*that street*!

"Bad Girls" was also inspired by life on the strip. I noticed "working women" always walking the streets. One day a young secretary, Nellie Prestwood, who worked in the PR department at Casablanca, went out for lunch and was mistaken by a policeman for a prostitute. She was a very pretty, well-dressed black woman who could just as easily have been mistaken for a model, but for some reason had been profiled as a hooker. She wasn't a bad girl in any sense of the word, but she was black and walking where the so-called bad girls walked, and because of it, the policeman had concluded that she was a prostitute. That was the incident that inspired "Bad Girls," which I wrote with Bruce, Joe, and Eddie at our friend Inky's studio in the Valley.

It made me very angry as a black woman, and I began to consider what kind of life it was for the women who actually were hookers. The song begins, "*Bad girls, sad girls, you see them out on the street at night, walkin', pickin' up all kind of strangers . . . if the price is right, but you can't score if your pocket's tight, but you want a good time. . . . Bad girls . . .*"

The whole point was that my friend was working a real job, but weren't the so-called bad girls doing so as well? Were they really all that different? The song wasn't a put-down. It was about sadness, the sadness of these girls' lives. As Sly Stone once wrote, *everybody is a star* or, at least, everyone wants to be one. Maybe the "bad girls" go about it in a way that is different from yours or mine, but they're just as real as we are. Anyway, I believe that God has a special place in His heart for bad girls who really love Him!

Once I had the idea, I went into the studio with the boys to see if they could help me figure out the chords. I already had the melody in my head. When I first took the demo to Neil, his re- action threw me for a loop. I was extremely excited when I walked in and told him he had to hear my new song. I put the demo on and he loved it. "Great," he said. He paused, then added, "But not for you. It's a perfect song for Cher."

I was so furious I almost flipped out! I knew he was trying to sign Cher to his label, which was all well and good. I love her a lot and think she's very beautiful and talented, but I wasn't about to give my song to her. I stood up to him and said, "I wrote this song for myself!" I then took the demo back and walked out.

I forgot all about "Bad Girls" until one day two years later. Steve Smith, the engineer from Rush Studio, found the song among the studio tapes. He quickly called me and said, "Donna, this is a hit record."

"I know," I said. "But Neil thinks it's better for Cher than me. I won't give it up, and he won't let me release it."

As soon as I heard myself say those words, I knew I had to do something. I couldn't let Neil or anyone else tell me that my own music wasn't right for me. How could such a thing be pos- sible? That was absurd!

"Why don't we pitch it directly to Giorgio?" he said. "Maybe he'll like it and ask Neil to reconsider his decision." I loved that idea.

Steve did just that. He gave the demo that I recorded with Bruce, Joe, and Eddie to Giorgio, who loved it so much he called and asked me to go right into the studio to work on it with him. We worked on it for days, but as much as I liked what he had done with it, I still felt there was something missing. I couldn't put my finger on what it was, but it sounded incomplete.

Finally, after repeated listenings, a light bulb went off in my head. "You know what, Giorgio? I want to throw a little cherry on the top of this cake."

"I'm listening," he said.

"How do you get the attention of a hooker? Especially if you're in a car on Sunset? Let's go back into the studio." He cued up the tape and I added the "toot-toot . . . ahh . . . beep-beep"s to the final mix. We took it back to Neil, who listened to it and agreed that it had to be released. It quickly soared to number one and went on to become the biggest hit of my career.

The success of that song made me realize something. The female singer-songwriters I most admired, such as Joni Mitchell, Carole King, and Aretha Franklin, were able to open a very private part of their inner lives and let you in. I've always found that kind of personalized songwriting to be too painful, which is why in my songwriting I preferred to create characters, like the "bad girl" whose story I told in that song. Of course it contains an essential element of a universal truth, but it is not about me. I always preferred to play the role of the observer rather than the lead.

"Bad Girls" gave me yet another huge hit single and album. It also meant I had to go back out on the road. We mounted the Summer Nights Dream Tour, which afforded me the opportunity to perform with Bruce and the Brooklyn Dreams. It was great having my friends onstage with me. We were like one big family. I'll never forget how excited Bruce was when we were booked for three nights to sold-out crowds at New York's Forest Hills tennis club, where the U.S. Open was played. Looking out at the sea of fans, it was as if all of New York had showed up to support us, especially from Bruce's hometown of Brooklyn.

Another memory of this engagement had nothing to do with the show. Susan had always arranged for me to leave a venue by going immediately from the stage into a waiting limo. However, this night, James Anderson and Bobby Stewart, my bodyguards, escorted me out the side door only to find that the waiting limo had been ushered away by the local police as it was violating a no-standing zone.

There I was in the middle of the street in full costume, wondering, Where's the car? I turned and saw a mob of fans running toward me. Susan immediately ran to the corner, flailing for a taxi. She managed to grab a cab, and my bodyguards pushed me into the taxi before I got trampled. The next thing I knew I was facedown on the floor of the taxi with my bodyguards on top of me as we fled the scene.

The public life of a singer who is on the charts, as I was at the time, becomes all-consuming and eventually takes everything out of you. If you're not extremely careful, if you don't keep a tight inventory on your own self-worth, you will wind up in some very strange places mentally and physically. That's why so many people in music take drugs or drink. It's their only way to cope, and it either kills them or forces them to look at the reality of their lives. The only way to survive the fame is to get control of your perspective on reality, and to do that you have to have a fairly strong frame of reference to the real world. Often it is extremely difficult to know whom you can trust.

My first day back at my office at Casablanca someone came up and congratulated me on my latest accomplishment—not the success of the tour, but the upcoming release of my new record. "Oh, we finished shipping your record today," he said. "It looks like you're going to have another big hit."

"What do you mean, you shipped my record?" I said. "I haven't been paid yet. They can't do that."

"Well, we've been shipping it for two weeks."

I went to the accounting department to find out what was going on, and they told me they had no record of anything with my name on it being shipped. I couldn't understand it. I went to Neil and asked him what was going on. He insisted he wasn't shipping anything.

I felt like I could trust almost no one at Casablanca anymore, that both I and the company had gotten too big, and the temptation for excess was overwhelming. I didn't know what to do next.

I turned to a man who subsequently took me under his wing and protected me like a father would his own child. That man was Norman Brokaw, vice president, at the time, of the William Morris Agency in Beverly Hills. I had phoned him after arriving in New York late one evening. When he heard my voice crying over the phone, he said he'd be right there. Early the next morning, there was a knock on my door— Norman had flown through the night to come to my aid.

My mentor, Norman Brokaw, chairman of the board of the William Morris Agency. *Photo by Harry Langdon; photo courtesy of Norman Brokaw*

He sat me down and informed me that he had long prepared for this day. Reaching into his pocket, he pulled out a glass prism that had been inscribed with the words "Donna Summer—Chairman of the Board." He stated that he worked for me and would do whatever I directed. He then gave me a pep talk that has stayed with me ever since. In an instant I grasped the fact that I was being advised by the same man who had brilliantly handled the careers of such women as Fanny Brice, Loretta Young, Susan Hayward, Kim Novak, Barbara Stanwyck, and the legendary Marilyn Monroe. I was in good hands and would be for more than twenty years, and for that, I will always love and respect him. He referred me to new counsel and gave me some very sound advice, not all of which I was ready for. But I needed to hear it anyway.

In my heart, I knew it was over between Neil and me. The very thought of that shattered my nerves because everything was so complicated. Casablanca was the center of my universe.

In the midst of all the chaos, Bruce remained my grounding force. We had managed to come together in the most beautiful and endearing way. From the beginning, Bruce had always been the one person who could see things clearly when I couldn't. We completely trusted each other's instincts, and he was always able to turn on my sanity switch.

We moved into a big house in Hancock Park that I thought resembled the Brooklyn Public Library. Not very long after, Bruce asked me to be his bride. It took about two and a half seconds for me to say *Yes, yes, yes!*

We were married July 16, 1980, the happiest day of my life.

Bruce and I on our wedding day! *Photo courtesy of the Sudano family archives*

Shortly thereafter we found out we were pregnant with our daughter Brooklyn.

However, happiness was not allowed to last for very long before the reality of the outside world crashed our little lovefest. In the midst of my ongoing legal battles with Neil, it was revealed that he was seriously ill. In fact, he was dying of cancer.

11

Hard for the Money

During the summer of 1979 I got the opportunity to record with the amazing Barbra Streisand. Singing with Barbra absolutely thrilled me, for a lot of reasons. Of course, the sheer pleasure of being in a studio with her was in and of itself a wonderful experience. However, it also afforded me the chance to make a very strong statement—to the public, to the industry, to Casablanca, and most of all to myself—that no matter what was going on with my business affairs, my talent was still intact. I was stronger than before—well, sort of—and I was not going to be bossed around any longer.

It was an important statement, for a lot of reasons. Despite all the hits I had had since "Love to Love You Baby," the enormous out-of-the-chute success of that recording had left too many people with the ongoing misconception that I was a one-hit wonder. It's true that the song had become, for better or worse, my signature at the time, and because of its strong impact

I had the good fortune to do what few artists besides Elvis and the Beatles had ever managed—that is, to ride the crest of the wave of new music. "Love to Love You Baby" caused a primal shift in Top 40 emphasis from rock to disco, or dance music. However, because that impact was so strong and lasting, no matter what else I did, it seemed I was destined to forever be known and remembered for one seventeen-minute moan-drenched song. Even the head of my own label was resistant to the idea that I might be able to have a career the morning after, and if he didn't go for it, who else would?

As a result, for all the time I was with Casablanca, I was asked to record music that never veered all that much from the initial boundaries that defined Donna Summer, Disco Queen. And because of it, no one in America had any real clue that I had an extensive and quite successful European background in live musical theater, or that I could actually sing other types of music.

As you might imagine, then, when the chance came to make a record with Barbra, I jumped at it, hoping to at last be able to stretch my commercial horizons and make a legitimate run as an across-the-board recording artist.

Here's how I came to record "Enough Is Enough" with Barbra Streisand. It was Paul Jabara who came up with the idea of doing the duet. Paul had won the Oscar for "Last Dance," and Charles Koppelman, Barbra's producer from Columbia, knew a good song when he heard it.

I happened to be renting William Wyler's Malibu beach house, spending some quality time with Bruce by the sea. I was on the beach when a call came from Paul saying he was going to be at Barbra's house that afternoon and wanted to stop by and say hello.

Barbra's place was just inside the famous "colony," that enclave of private beach where lots of celebrities lived. Wyler's house, like his career, was just outside the colony, close enough that I could put one foot in the colony and the other on Wyler's own porch.

When Paul arrived, we had some coffee, talked for a while, and then he asked me if he could play this song he'd written. I said sure and put his demo on. I told him I really liked it, and that's when he let me know that Barbra was going to record the song. Great, I thought to myself, you can't miss with her. Then he asked if it would be okay for him to suggest that I record it with her. I was floored. I'd love to, I told him. Who wouldn't want to record with Barbra Streisand? "Great," he said. He gave me a quick hug and took off on foot down the beach, leaving his car in my driveway.

A little while later he called to say that Barbra loved the idea and that he was coming back to pick up his car and me along with it, and bring us both to her place.

The next thing I knew, I was at Ms. Streisand's house. She was a complete delight, and it didn't take long for us to fall into a nice conversation. Before I left, Paul sat down at her grand piano and played "Enough Is Enough" for the both of us, comically doing all the parts. What a thrill for me!

The next day Paul began to look for a place for us to record the song. We wound up trying four different studios. In one the sound wasn't right for Paul, in another it wasn't right for me, in still another Barbra didn't like it, and the fourth seemed wrong to all three of us. Once we finally found a studio we all agreed on, it was smooth sailing.

Almost.

✳

The afternoon of our scheduled final session also happened to be the day after my last performance of an eight-night sold-out run at the Universal Amphitheatre. I was completely exhausted, having partied all night after the show. The next day, Barbra and I were at the studio, having a great time making jokes and teasing each other, until it was time to sing. Barbra was doing her part, and when it was my turn, I came in for the high note behind her lead, but for some reason I couldn't get enough air. I tried to hold the note anyhow, but I was really more tired from my eight-night run than I'd realized, and before I knew it, I'd fallen off my stool and passed out. My lights went out so fast I don't even remember hitting the floor.

Here's the best part: when I came to and opened my eyes a few seconds later, Barbra was still holding her note! I could have died. It was so long! It was only when she finished that she turned and asked me, "Donna, are you all right?" in a way only Barbra speaks. I said I was, got up, cleared my throat, and finished the session.

I feel blessed to have had the opportunity to sing with a woman of such immense talent. I've always loved her music, and what can I say? It's a wonderful feeling of opportunity and privilege to have the chance to perform with one of your true heroes. To me, she is truly great!

At the time I was recording with Barbra, I happened to have the number one and number two songs on the pop charts, "Bad Girls" and "Dim All the Lights." Even so, Neil went ahead and authorized Columbia to immediately release "Enough Is Enough" as a single. He had promised me he would make Columbia wait at least a couple of weeks, until my two records had had their full moment, and then only as part of the *Greatest Hits* album first, before the single became available. I was furious. When I asked him why he'd gone back on his word, he made up some story about how the record had been "stolen" and put on the air without his permission and therefore Columbia had to rush-release it. It was a big hit; I knew it, he knew it, and he knew I knew it.

This was the turning point, as though divine Providence were waving a hand in my face saying, "Enough is enough." Sure enough, "Enough Is Enough" knocked "Dim All the Lights" out of going to the number one spot. Mind you, I'm not overlooking the fact that I now had three songs in the top five. That part of it was wonderful, and you could rightly call me crazy to have thought anything else. It was Neil's betrayal that undid me. "Dim All the Lights" meant something to me beyond chart position and sales. It was the first hit song that I had written the music and words to alone. My personal goal of achieving a number one song as a singer-songwriter had been short-circuited. To me, my song was an accomplishment, but to Neil it seemed to be "product," and product *only*. This cut me deeply.

That did it for me. I wanted out—out of the company, out of my professional relationship with Neil, out of Beverly Hills. My time in Malibu had given me a fresh perspective on the whole L.A. music-biz scene. Then David Geffen came back into my life.

✳

David Geffen is the genius and innovator in every field of entertainment he is involved in, and one of the shrewdest businessmen ever to hit Hollywood. I'd first met him at a party in New York City at Halston's Manhattan town house. Halston entertained in the reception area, a beautiful open space that led to a long stairway, with dozens of gorgeous models and celebrities, music playing everywhere, and wonderful food and cocktails served all through the evening. David is a world-class charmer, and from that first night he tried everything in his arsenal to convince me to join the new label he was putting together once my contract with Casablanca was up.

Having sold Asylum to Warner Music, he was now planning to start Geffen Records. The great thing about David is how he is always able to focus on exactly what he wants, go after it, and not give up until he gets his way, although in my case I was a real test of his endurance.

I thought I would be with Neil and Casablanca for my entire career. Eventually, as things went downhill at Casablanca, I accepted David's offer to join Geffen Records. From the beginning, I was so comfortable with him it was second nature for me to go over to his house in Beverly Hills to play his piano, write

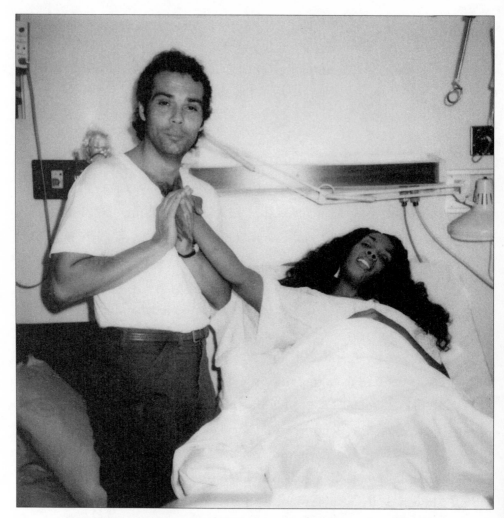

With Bruce, goofing around while I was in labor expecting Amanda, 1982. *Photo courtesy of the Summer archives*

music, or just hang out. He was that way with all the acts he handled, including Linda Ronstadt, the Eagles, and Jackson Browne, to name a few. One afternoon at Geffen's house, song-writer Bruce Roberts and I wrote a song called "Sometimes Like Butterflies." I didn't stop creating in spite of all the prob-lems plaguing the business side of my career.

✳

It took a long time for me to finalize my differences with Casablanca. In the interim I recorded *The Wanderer* album with Giorgio for Geffen Records. I recorded a second album, which was canned, and then David had the idea to phone Quincy Jones to see if he would produce my next album. Quincy had the challenge, however, of producing the record during the time I was pregnant with my third child, Amanda, battling morning, noon, and night sickness. Every day it seemed like my days got longer and my breath got shorter and shorter. I was tired and cranky and pregnant. Need I say more? Quincy—or Q as we called him—was ever positive, a real trouper. He hung in there until I could accomplish what we had set out to do. He chal-lenged me to sing the most incredible jazz song, "Lush Life." After having to sing it so many times, I learned what the term "paying your dues" really meant.

It was Q's genius to team me up with Bruce Springsteen. Quincy asked him if he would write a song for the new album. Shortly thereafter, "The Boss" showed up at my front door with a new song he'd written for me, called "Protection." I loved it. I'd seen him many times at his concerts, swinging his guitar from side to side as he strutted across the stage. Now there he was sitting in my little music room, humbly singing his song just for me. Wow, somebody pinch me! And my husband was his number one fan. Now, that was a day to remember. I received another Grammy nomination for Female Rock Vocalist for "Protection." Thank you, Bruce and Q!

Quincy also came up with the idea of recording the Vangelis–Jon Anderson song "State of Independence" as an epic with a cast of voices that included Michael Jackson, Kenny Loggins, James Ingram, Brenda Russell, and others. This trend-setting song helped pave the way for such future epics as "We Are the World."

Then word reached me that Neil had died. He was only thirty-nine years old when his battle with cancer took his life. I was devastated. No matter what had gone on between us, and regardless of all the false information and speculative garbage that has since been printed about our relationship, I had then and still do have a special place in my heart for him, and I always will. I wept and sang for him at his funeral. It was the end of an era.

My attorney, Don Engel, worked out a settlement with the executives at Polygram who had since bought out the remaining fifty percent of Casablanca. In return, I had to deliver one more album to Polygram. As long as I was going to do it, even though I wasn't in a particularly good frame of mind, I set about making it the best record I knew how to make.

The title song, "She Works Hard for the Money," was based partly on my ongoing fascination with the working woman. I saw it as a follow-up to "Bad Girls" that also offered some insight as to how I was feeling about the whole music industry.

I was on my way to a Grammy after-party for Julio Iglesias, having skipped the ceremony because of an upset stomach. I had to go straight to the ladies' room as soon as I arrived at Chasen's Restaurant, in Beverly Hills. When I got to the rest room I saw an attractive attendant sitting by a small television set, fast asleep. I looked at the woman and felt a wave of sympathy. This poor woman had to be cooped up in the bathroom all night long. I blurted out, "She works hard for the money." Instantly I felt some strange excitement race right through me, and I said it again: "She works hard for the money." I asked my manager, Susan, to get me a piece of paper—toilet paper, anything! I had to write the words to what clearly was becoming a song. As I scratched out the words, I watched all the fancily dressed women come and go, in and out of the stalls, dousing themselves with perfume and gossiping, oblivious to the lady trying to catch a few seconds of sleep.

I tried to envision what her day-to-day life was like, how this must be her second job because she was obviously so worn out. In an instant I made up a whole life for her in my head, which became the basis for my song and album. I came to find out later that she had a good day job at Cedars-Sinai as a lab technician. She made a good living, but with no husband and a son she was putting through college, she had taken on this second job.

I phoned my producer, Michael Omartian, the next morning and sang him the melody and some of the lyrics I had written at Chasen's. He loved it and immediately put down a track in less than twenty-four hours. I went to his studio the next day and wrote the rest of the words to the song at the microphone. Onetta, the rest-room attendant, let me put her picture on the back cover of the album with me.

I was already in the studio working on an album for Geffen Records when Polygram released "She Works Hard for the Money." To everyone's surprise, it became a big hit. The song became an anthem for many working-class people, and the single shot up the charts. Because no one had anticipated its success, it threw everyone at both labels into a king-sized tizzy! Polygram was upset because I was back on top and they had let me out of my contract. That meant whatever follow-up was to be had, it wasn't going to be for them. They had a Top Ten lame duck on their hands.

But Geffen Records was also upset because I had a hit with my old label. They felt I should have saved that material for them, especially after it went on to become one of the biggest albums I'd had in a long time. Who would have thought that by this time next year, I would be nominated for a Grammy as Best Pop Female Vocalist for "She Works Hard for the Money"? I was even asked to perform it as the coveted opening number for the award show, to which I gladly agreed.

On the way to the show, before the live broadcast, I got stuck in a mile-long line of stretch limos. I was dressed in full costume, ready for the show, and getting very, very impatient. Anxious about being late and overcome by stress, my body reacted and demanded that I immediately find a lavatory.

The ladies of "mass construction." Left to right: Denise Eppolito, Pat Naderhoff, and Susan Munao. *Photo courtesy of Pat Naderhoff*

My bodyguard directed the driver to the nearest McDonald's, where he jumped out of the limo and practically carried me to the ladies' room. Everyone inside recognized me in my waitress costume from the album cover and began chanting "hard for the money," which I could hear in my stall.

After finishing, I raced back to the limo, and we took off down the wrong side of the street. I finally jumped from the limo and ran a block at full speed through a crowd. There I was in full costume sprinting wildly, weaving around and between people, trying desperately to get to the Grammys, where I was scheduled to perform in minutes!

I arrived panting, desperately out of breath and more than a little disoriented, with only moments to spare. Nonetheless, I danced onto the stage and completed the opening number live on network broadcast, paying homage to the credo "The show must go on."

That was the music business. I had a hit, and everyone was upset about it. It was enough to make me miss Neil.

✳

After the success of "She Works Hard for the Money," things began to go downhill at Geffen Records. A rumor was printed that I was homophobic, which caused unnecessary pain for my fans and for me. David Geffen publicly denounced the story and urged me to do the same. While we disagreed on the type and level of response, I was grateful for his support. I had been the victim of many false rumors in the past. (Remember the rumor that I was a transvestite?) To me it had always seemed pointless to dignify rumors with a public response, and so my inclination was to ignore the false allegations. My interactions with people have always been based solely upon their character, integrity, and ability, irrespective of their race, gender, sexual preference, or religious beliefs.

As it turned out, my move to Geffen Records was not that successful. It looked like a great marriage on paper but turned out to be not so great in real life. When it became clear that we were unable to re-create the kind of magic I'd had with Neil, David Geffen and I both agreed it would be in our best interests if I left the label while we were still friends. I apologized to David that it didn't work out and left Geffen Records. Our parting was amicable, and David was very gracious.

Still, the split with Geffen Records hit me hard, enough to trigger a resurgence of old insecurities. I became disillusioned and depressed. I realized I didn't have a lot of real friends outside the small world of the music biz. I found myself more than once turning my head and looking for Neil, eager to ask his advice about what I should do next. But, of course, he wasn't there. It secretly broke my heart. I needed to see Neil so I could tell him that in spite of our differences, I was grateful to have had him in my life and that I wouldn't have been who I was without him. Mistakes are not more important than the people who make them, and forgiveness, as Don Henley says, is "the heart of the matter."

12

The Connection

During all my years on the pop charts, I was never into the excessive materialism normally attached to success. I wore what my managers wanted me to onstage, but in my personal life I was used to a more European lifestyle. I am, by nature, a contemplative human being, with no great need for the outer glitz. Early on, Neil thought I should be driving a Mercedes-Benz, the then-requisite "I am a star" car of L.A., and bought me one, along with a BMW. I would rather understate than overstate my success, and thus I still preferred my Jeep. I never felt the need to define myself by what I had—I always believed that what I had was defined by *me*.

I had financially exceeded my childhood dreams. I had everything I needed—everything, that is, except *myself*! *I* was what was missing in my life! I was stranded as an artist, isolated, emotionally and spiritually bereft, and prisoner to the most carnal of lifestyles. Paul Jabara wrote a song called "Something's

Amanda's christening at the Resorts International hotel in Atlantic City.
Left to right: Brooklyn (age two), Lou and Madge Sudano (Bruce's parents), me, Mimi, Bruce, my mother, and my father holding Amanda.
Photo courtesy of the Sudano family archives

Missing in My Life," which summed up how I felt at that time. The only thing I desired was to somehow find a way to reconnect to myself, to be able to reach back across the years to a time when it was *only* about me getting on that stage and singing my heart out, when it was *only* about showing everyone I had a unique gift. I wanted to get back to that ordinary girl who'd sung that day in church. Where was she anyway? What had happened to her? Where had she gone? What was her name? Perhaps this is a place that all artists come to sooner or later.

The voice I kept hearing in my head was asking the same question: "Where am I?" It wasn't talking about our home in Hancock Park either. I had no answer. Each chapter in my life had played itself out and had become a part of my past, like the skin of a shedding snake. All fine and good, except I was not that hollow, discarded shell but the creature who had once lived inside. The skin was history; the creature was in search of tomorrow.

In 1979, I invited my sister Dara to come stay with me in our guesthouse in Hancock Park while we were rehearsing to go out on the road. I loved having family around. One beautiful L.A. September afternoon not long after her arrival, Dara came into the garden and sat down next to me at the table. I had been sitting alone amid my thoughts, sipping a cup of herbal tea. She said she had something she wanted to tell me. "Donna," she began, in a low and serious voice, "I've met a man and I've been praying with him. I think you should meet him. He's sweet and spiritual, and I think he can help you find the way out of your problems."

"My problems," I repeated slowly. So that was what Dara thought was bothering me! I shook my head and laughed out loud for the first time in a while. The last thing I thought I needed was a new friend. I felt like telling her that in case she didn't know it, I already believed in God, thank you very much! I had no particular inclination to meet anyone, especially someone who fancied himself some sort of guru.

The Jonestown nightmare was still vivid in my mind, and I was more than a little wary of self-styled spiritual leaders, for my sister as well as myself. I used to get letters from people all the time saying that they were praying for me. These would always offend me. I'd feel as if they were condescending, that these people were trying to help me atone for something they felt I'd done, and yet they had never met me and knew very little about my real life. My point of view was so tilted that I was certain everyone was out to get something from me. Including my sister's friend.

Especially my sister's friend!

As I finished my tea, I told her that not only did I *not* want to meet this fellow, but I didn't even want him coming on my property to visit *her.* Of course, I didn't realize at the time that Dara could read me like a book, and what she'd read had alarmed her. She was not someone who easily dispensed advice to others. What did she mean anyway?

I had a great career. As a matter of fact, I was right in the middle of an exciting week. I was in rehearsals for my first network television special for ABC while also preparing for the live portion of that show at the Hollywood Bowl. Twiggy was a guest star on the show. I was also working with my old friend Robert Guillaume. He and I went back to my Vienna Volksoper days, when the two of us had worked together in *Porgy and Bess*. We would bum around with the cast back then in the artsy European cafés, drinking caffe lattes and eating Sacher torte. He was currently doing well in his career, costarring as a butler with Billy Crystal on the popular TV sitcom *Soap*. The show also gave me an opportunity to involve Mimi in my work in a unique way as I sang "Mimi's Song" on camera to her. I had all the money I'd ever need, a new, beautiful house, and, most important, a wonderfully cool and comfortable man in my life.

"I'm fine. I'm fine. . . . Leave me alone, I'm fine," I said.

But was I?

✳

The truth, of course, was that my demons had never really gone completely away. They were hiding in a closet in the back of my mind. Deep down inside I believed I was still ugly and awkward. Deep down inside I had not forgiven my past mistakes and was still ashamed of many things I had done. And, yes, she was right; I was in pain. I needed help.

I'd wake up in the morning and, while still in bed, throw my arms straight into the air and stay that way for no reason, sometimes for nearly an hour, as if I was trying to reach God. With my hands above my head I'd pray, and ask Him, "*Please . . . God . . . tell . . . me . . . what . . . to . . . do.*" This had been going on for weeks, even before my sister approached me about this man. Before getting out of bed, I'd longingly wait to hear the

Family Christmas, circa 1983–1984. I am holding Amanda, Mimi is in the middle, and Bruce is holding Brooklyn. *Photo by Rosario Argueta*

voice of God whisper in my ear, *"I'm still here, Donna . . . I'm still here,"* but for some reason I could not hear His voice.

I was breaking down from the inside. I'd developed stomach ulcers and could barely eat. I was maxed out on all my medications, and the sleeping pills weren't working. I stayed awake for days at a time. I lived in constant fear that my heart problems would resurface and throw me into a hospital or worse. I was starting to have lapses in memory and constant anxiety attacks. On top of it, my already overcrowded schedule was getting more and more insane. I had occasional thoughts of suicide again, even on the medication. Maybe that's what I couldn't hide from Dara? Weeks passed this way, and finally I felt I had absolutely nowhere else to turn. I went back to my sister. Out of desperation, which was barely covered by my unusually cocky manner, I said to her, "Okay. Where is this guy?! I want to meet him."

✳

She invited him over the next day. My first impression was the complete opposite of what I had expected, which was some sort of fast-talking, wild, religious weirdo. Instead, here was a plainly dressed, very humble man in his thirties, almost my peer. After talking with him for a while I thought to myself, He's the real thing. At one point he turned and said to me in a calm, soothing voice, "Look, Donna, I know you're having some problems, and I just want to tell you that no matter what has happened in your life, God will forgive you and God will help you. Let's pray." And I prayed what's called the "Sinner's

Prayer" with him. For whatever reason, I quickly yielded to him, taken totally by surprise by his kind and gentle manner.

During our prayer a sense of elation came over me that was beyond any spiritual experience I had ever had before. I felt as if a ton of bricks were lifted off my shoulders. This feeling blew into me like a hurricane, through my whole body, taking with it anything and everything that was troubling me. At that moment I felt all my priorities shift, the darkness disappear, and my entire being bathed in light.

I started repeating this one word, *Abba,* over and over again. I had no idea at the time that the word meant Father in Hebrew, and I had no idea why I was saying it, but it kept coming out of my mouth. I began to cry as I repeated it over and over again: "Abba, Abba, Abba . . ." Through a flurry of tears I could feel something shaking in my deepest being, and I was at once free. *Abba, Abba, Abba.* The light came shining into my spirit, and it was a familiar light, although one I hadn't seen for a long, long time. *Abba, Abba, Abba . . .* It was the same light I had seen shining on that stranger down on the Bowery that night so very long ago!

That day in 1979, in my house in Hancock Park, was the day I was finally filled by God's Holy Spirit and gloriously born again.

The man explained to me, "Being born again means simply that; a person is first born of the flesh, from the womb of the mother. The second birth is to the birth of the Spirit of God." He continued, "It is the moment of one's infilling with the spirit. And once that happens, everything changes, because you now have God's Spirit also within you for the rest of your life. To have God within you is to have faith in God. And, ultimately, to have faith in God is to have asked Him into your life, to have faith in what He created you to be, and His ability to fulfill it."

Most people call upon God when they're having a personal crisis, when they have nowhere else to turn, when they think they need special recognition or a special favor. What they don't realize is that making a personal commitment to Him means you are *always* connected to God, and He is always there for you in your heart, in your soul, in your spirit, in your *life*. For many years I had carried a secret burden of things I had done that were moral lapses of behavior, with no way to cope with the shame. The bad feelings from my past carved themselves into my psyche. As a result, I lived with this impending fear of doom, a fatalism that controlled my life until the day I accepted Jesus into it, and realized that since God was really the one I felt I had betrayed, He was the *only* One who could forgive me.

The day I had my conversion was the first day of the rest of my life. I knew I was forgiven and free. I knew at last that God truly loved me. That day I had spoken His name and He had spoken mine. In an instant I was changed. Faith, I realized, was the key to my future. Without faith, it is impossible to please God, and therefore to please yourself. From that day on, I renewed my faith in God and was ready to deal with life from a new, more positive perspective. This choice changed everything for me. And for the first time in years, the troubled voices in my head were silent and the dark shadows over my heart disappeared.

Each step had brought me forward to a new and better place. Not long after my surrender to God, my creative focus returned, better than ever. I was vibrating with life, and it caused a primal shift in my emphasis and focus. It led me to want to make my life even more private. I did not want to retire from show business or anything like that, but I wanted to become more selective in how I led my life, so that I would never again have to pay the sacrificial price for fame. In other words, while I no longer felt married to my public, I did want to extend generous visitation rights!

I began attending a Bible-study class to become more spiritually centered, and I made an effort to take as much time as I needed to get to know God and God's word, which takes years of studying. It's a journey that once begun never stops until you're studying in His presence. Thank God that I had committed my life to Him before the next phase of my life began to unfold.

✳

I had taken a Memorial Day engagement in Las Vegas at the Hilton and was thrilled to be playing there again. I had put together a brand-new show, complete with new costumes, new sets, and new music. I was excited to have the opportunity to break in the show with a live audience. Everyone was buzzing about with the scintillating excitement that only a new show can bring. We went on the first night and struck pay dirt! The reviews in the coming days would be some of the best in my career.

Dara, Mary, and the conductor Mari Falcone with me (second from left) after a show at the Las Vegas Hilton. *Photo courtesy of the Sudano family archives*

The morning after opening night Bruce took a call from Susan Munao while I still lay in bed. A few minutes later I felt him sit on the edge of the bed. I turned to see his grave look, which caused me immediate concern. My stomach sank, and I could feel my heart starting to beat faster. He began to tell me that something terrible had happened and that my sister Dara's husband, Gilbert, had been in a car crash with their two best friends and that couple's son. The son was driving during the night while Gilbert and the couple slept. No one was wearing a seat belt. The vehicle was only traveling thirty miles per hour when the axle suddenly broke, flipping the car numerous times and throwing everyone but the son from the vehicle. The son survived, but Gilbert and the others did not make it.

I started screaming, "THIS CANNOT BE HAPPEN-ING!" Bruce grabbed me and held me tightly. He was in shock too. He'd been very good friends with Gilbert; after all, Gilbert was his brother-in-law too. We sat on the bed, dazed, speech-less, and crying. When we came to our senses I tried to find my assistant, Gina, who, unbeknownst to me, was suffering from severe stomach pain and needed to be taken to the hospital.

Spontaneous chaos ensued as a horde of people descended upon my suite—my sisters Dara and Mary, along with Gerardo (Mary's husband), Susan, Bobby Stewart (one of my body-guards), and the band and crew. For hours, it seemed, we walked around in a thick fog.

The hotel insisted I finish my weekend commitment of four remaining shows, two per day, which I performed through my oblique numbness in an altered state. It was actually a good thing that we were all able to get together and pray through this time. We called ahead to L.A. to prepare for the funerals, and we went home on Monday to bury our lost loved ones. I cried my eyes dry. Losing Gilbert was a new pain, a pain like I had never had before.

It was a growing experience. I was amazed that even though we were all emotionally taxed and devastated by this experience, once we had weathered the initial shock we seemed to dwell in a form of suspended peace. In the coming days we were certainly going to need it.

My sister Linda's baby had died of SIDS just months before Gilbert's accident, and almost a year later, her husband, Andre, was also killed in another car crash. Then my brother's son, Morgan, accidentally shot himself in the heart and was instantly killed; my cousin Richard was shot by the police; and my father's brother, Solomon, was killed by a hit-and-run driver. Was this some kind of spiritual endurance test? It got to the point where I was afraid to pick up the phone for fear I was going to hear more bad news. I also lost other close friends during this time.

In spite of everything, my faith in God grew. He was holding me up and carrying me through. I'm not saying that our circumstances were easier; I just seemed to be getting stronger. My emotions didn't fluctuate like they had in the past. My nerves seemed more stable, and now it seemed I was able to handle more emotional responsibility. The child in me was finally coming of age.

13

The Gift

Ever since I could remember, I had wanted to live on a farm. I'd once made a video for Geffen Records in which I had to ride a moped along a street. I kept stopping at the gate to a particular house. I fell so in love with that property! Throughout the video shoot I kept seeing this beautiful landscape, like a painting. There were numerous sun-drenched bales of freshly rolled hay neatly arranged in an open field. The view transported me to the very "bliss of solitude" Wordsworth may have felt when he penned his famous poem "Daffodils." I was completely taken. All at once, I was frozen in time by the awesome simplicity of that moment. I had found another missing piece of my soul. I was home.

For days, I could not get the vision out of my mind, until finally I decided I had to, had to, had to go back and see it again, hoping maybe there was a house in the vicinity I might be able to purchase. Now that we had decided to move, I called my real

Amanda and Brooklyn with Bruce on the farm in Thousand Oaks, California—"the good life." *Photo courtesy of the Sudano family archives*

estate broker and had him put together a list of all the available houses in Thousand Oaks, and sure enough the house from the video was on it. I went back the next day to take a closer look. It had an enclosed courtyard and an Olympic-sized pool in the back, with a cabana, huge oak trees, an underground wine cellar, and several more buildings, including two guesthouses, a pavilion, and tons of storage, all on fifty-six acres. Bruce could have his very own recording studio and I could have my atelier. And there was enough space for all the animals I wanted. It was perfect; all the things we had wanted and that I had prayed for were on this property.

My manager, Susan Munao, knew the owner, Jimmy Guercio, who was the former producer of the rock band Chicago. She called him directly. When Jimmy discovered our interest, he worked out an agreeable deal. Sure enough, within a month or so, we acquired our dream house.

While we remodeled the house, I turned my energies inward and got even deeper into reading the Bible. The Bible had always been a very difficult book for me to understand. Now I promised myself I would read ten Scriptures a day, without fail. And I increased my prayer time. I always reserved some time every day to pray to God while tending my garden. One of the great things about gardening is that it involves cutting flowers to ensure they bloom larger and fuller. That was an interesting parallel to our lives. This was precisely what I had done with my career. Even though I was no longer performing as often as I used to, by cutting back I'd strengthened my musical as well as my spiritual roots, and I'd acquired better endurance in the process.

Now I prayed for God to be able to harness my spiritual energy, to gain the ability to do all the things required of me. By recognizing God's strength, I had gained more of my own.

The change that came over me was noticeable to everyone, but not in the same way it was to me. A lot of people thought I had retired, left the stage—as in "Elvis has left the building"—whatever; but what had really changed was my perspective on life and my sense of purpose. I stopped making external stimuli my focal point. Instead, I directed my eyes inward and started looking at my own soul.

Life on the farm was invaluable. It brought new sounds, new colors, new experiences to my life. Things I'd feared in the city were no longer present. But there were new fears: black widow and tarantula spiders, skunks, scorpions, rodents of all sizes, lizards, snakes, killer bee swarms, and much more. Finally those fears got the better of me, and we moved out for a few days while an exterminator tented the place. I couldn't stand the thought of anything creeping around in my home. Believe me, on fifty-six acres there was plenty of room, so we would be able to cohabitate.

One night not that long after Bruce and I moved into the farm, we were lying in bed warming up to what we thought would be a very romantic evening, when suddenly out of the still, black night we heard a very disturbing sound: *Mooooo. Moooo.*

Startled, we sat up and looked out the window where the sound was coming from. To Bruce's horror, the cows he had just purchased were now roaming all over the farm, and it was up to this Brooklyn-born city slicker to round up the cattle.

He leaped out of bed and jumped into his boots, forgetting his pants. Somehow he managed to pull on a shirt and, on the way out the front door, grab a whip. "YEE HAW, YEE HAW," he yelled at the top of his lungs. Try as he might, the cows were impervious to his commands. In defiance, they just turned their butts to him, flipped their tails, and ignored him. After much whip cracking, Bruce finally got the cows moving.

By the time I caught up with him, the cattle were racing down our driveway, toward the street. We had to stop them. So I jumped into my Ford Bronco and raced along the hillside, avoiding the road so as not to trigger the automatic gate, but the gate opened anyway. Driving faster than the cows could run— about ninety miles an hour—I cut them off just as one little heifer escaped past the gate. Bruce jumped to the rescue and rounded her up while I rounded up the others with the Bronco. Out of breath I said to Bruce, "*Wow,* that was *utter* chaos." With a Brooklyn accent, he turned to me and said, "You *butter* believe it, baby." We burst out laughing. The next day, one of the cows gave birth to a beautiful baby calf. We were now officially farmers. Yee haw.

✳

While living in Thousand Oaks, Bruce and I became friendly with Sylvester Stallone, who invited us to the reception for his wedding to Brigitte Nielsen. Sly was just getting into his painting. He was very enthusiastic, and his large canvases inspired me to try some of my own that size. I shared that interest with him, something I had dabbled in all the way back in my days in

Munich. I, too, had recently gone back to painting, but I was doing a lot of small oils that took forever to complete. I loved painting for a lot of reasons, but none more than its lasting physical presence. The difference between painting and performing for me is that at the end of a concert there is nothing left except a sense of elation that diminishes with time. It is a completely ethereal experience. The music comes out of me, it's heard, and then it's gone. With painting, whatever I put down on that canvas is there when I wake up the next day, and forever. In that way it's more like a recording than an event, more permanent, like a live album of a show rather than the show itself. *And it is exclusively mine!* There are no producers, no directors, no engineers, no industry moguls, no agents, no managers, no collaborators, no trend to have to follow. It's only me and that empty canvas, mine to fill up any way I choose. That's why for many years I never showed anyone my paintings. I painted for me, and for me only.

But it would drive me nuts that I could never seem to finish many paintings, because I was always being distracted by other things. It wasn't until the day at Sly's house that I found my solution. Sly showed me some of his abstracts. He had life-sized canvases everywhere, and something clicked. I went out the next day and got some really big canvases. Sure enough, it proved to be a real turning point in my art. I realized for the first time that I had been thinking too small, and it was interfering with my ability to express myself. Thank you, Sly.

This was a revelation I was able to expand into all areas of my career and my life. I began to realize that my hits had caused me to narrow the realm of my recording possibilities. I had been thinking too small for too much of the time. There is an expression in the Bible that says, "Your gift will make room for you." I needed to enlarge my thinking to allow my gift to give me that room. I started to paint feverishly, day in and day out, and try all kinds of experiments with color, textures, topics, and subjects.

I felt free. I was very happy indeed.

One day I threw a big party for Bruce. In the process of all the preparation, I piled all of my paintings in a hallway for safekeeping. Ceil Kasha, a dear friend of mine, discovered my paintings that night. An interior decorator, Ceil quickly located me and dragged me back to the hallway. She immediately asked if any of my artwork was available for her to sell to her clients. Right then, David Duclon, currently one of the television producers of *Family Matters,* joined our conversation and promptly offered me money on the spot for one of the paintings. I was stunned. I had never thought of selling my paintings and, consequently, had never assigned a monetary value to them. The running joke was that I would have to die first before my paintings would be worth anything.

Soon after the party I held my first exhibition, at the Javits Center in New York City. On the evening of the opening, Ceil and I were invited to several artists' receptions. I was exhausted, having stood for hours at the Javits Center. But Ceil insisted that we make all the parties. Finally, we arrived very late at the Circle Fine Arts party. We walked in and, to my surprise, there were Jack and Carolyn Solomon, a couple I had met several years before when Gunther was working on his lithos in their atelier in Manhattan.

They raced over to me, and we immediately began to recall all the great fun we'd had in the past. Jack and Carolyn would eventually become my art representatives and sell many of my paintings and lithos in their galleries. Little had I suspected that the time I'd spent hanging out with artists in Munich and Vienna would someday serve as the foundation for a second career in the visual arts. That was a great lesson.

Thanks, Ceil. "Love ya, babe."

✳

When we first settled into the farm, I decided that my children needed to get closer to one another. In one of our bedrooms, I put in two queen-sized four-poster canopy beds and had all three—Mimi, Brooklyn, and the newest member of our family, Amanda—in the same room. I wanted them to experience the joy of being sisters and to strengthen their bonds by getting to know one another. I had them sleep together in the same room for two years, until I was satisfied they were comfortably integrated into one another's lives. Only then did I allow my oldest, Mimi, to have her own room. The younger two opted to continue to share the room, which pleased me greatly.

I got into the habit of praying for my daughters in advance for everything they were about to do. Not just on the day before but often years ahead of the actual event. Looking back now, twenty years later, I can honestly say that God answered my prayers.

✳

It so happened that Sophia Loren, Carlo Ponti, and their sons lived on the same street we did, and we all became quite friendly. I have to say Sophia deserves a special mention. She is a unique woman who taught me a great deal about life, food, children, and a woman's role as a mother and wife from her quintessentially Italian perspective.

I don't think I'm going to surprise anyone when I say that she is disarmingly human. She was then and has been most of her life all woman *and* all mother at the same time. She is living proof that one role can embrace the other. I absolutely adore her! She's got a serious case of "Womanity!" *Womanity* is a word that was inspired by Sophia. It refers to the attributes of a woman and the compassion of humanity all rolled into one.

That was something she showed me more clearly than anyone else. So many women believe that if they allow themselves to act "motherly" they will lose some aspect of their femininity, which couldn't be further from the truth. If I learned anything from Sophia, it was that I could be a mother and still be perceived as sensuous.

Somehow in America we've had this notion that if a woman works full-time and has any degree of success, she becomes more masculine than the "little woman" waiting with makeup and perfume for her husband to come home from the office. Sophia showed me that having a successful career didn't mean one was less of a woman.

One day Sophia called me and said, "Donna, would you

like to come over and have lunch today?" I said, "Of course. What should I wear?" She laughed softly and said, "Anything, a pair of shorts. Whatever." I said, "Oh great, that's just what I'm wearing." Off I went, just like that. When I arrived, she was standing in her doorway fully made up, in a beautiful floral-patterned yellow designer cocktail dress, looking drop-dead gorgeous. I couldn't believe it!

"Sophia," I said, "you said dress casually." At that moment she leaned against the door, smiled in CinemaScope, and said, *"After all, Donna, I am Sophia . . ."* We broke out laughing! It was such a funny moment to me, but there was also a funda-mental lesson to be learned. She never felt the need to sacrifice any part of herself to satisfy anyone else. She was so comfortable with who she was that she could actually make fun of herself in that way. By the same token she allowed you to be yourself. She was all glamour, all humor, all gardener, all mother, and be-cause of it, all woman.

Sophia and Carlo had a garden that they kept in beautiful condition. At this time in the mid-eighties, it was difficult to find fresh arugula in southern California. Sophia and I grew it, and were always sharing our arugula with each other. She even brought seeds from Italy for me to plant in my garden. We shared lots of little things.

Carlos, her cook and butler, would sometimes come over to get some fresh herbs from my garden, and later in the afternoon he would show up with an entire cooked dinner for my whole family, soup to nuts—pasta, chicken, vegetables, dessert, every-thing, all courtesy of Sophia's own kitchen! *Wow!!!* And let me tell you, the food was better than that of any Italian restaurant in L.A. simply because it was the real thing and it was truly Italian, cooked with so much love.

One night I invited Sophia and her family for dinner. Oh goodness, what was I thinking? Sophia, Carlo, and their sons, Carlo and Eduardo, were to come over to our house for dinner. Wow! For the occasion I invited my manager, Susan, who is Italian, to join us and help my cook, Rosa, prepare dinner.

Rosa, a native of El Salvador, could cook great South American cuisine and any other style of food, if taught, with such skill. This night was to be her Italian culinary boot camp.

Bruce's parents were staying with us, and Madge, my mother-in-law, who is also Italian, decided that she had to get in the kitchen. His dad helped out as well.

Everything was going fine, except that my entire family, my manager, and my staff were in the kitchen, working their tails off, while I was the only one in the living room playing hostess. It was an informal occasion, and I was trying to keep the evening light and breezy. But everyone in the kitchen was freaking out like schoolkids, because *Sophia Loren* was in the house and we were cooking Italian style!

The dinner turned into a fiasco. Every few seconds, someone else's head peeked out from the kitchen doors to catch a glimpse of her. I could hear plates dropping on the floor, and loud yelling. All the dishes came out wrong. What should have been al dente pasta ended up al mushe, and after a few moments of panic on my part at the beginning of the dinner, I just threw my hands up in exasperation and broke out laughing. Sophia laughed along with me, and from that moment on we all had the best time.

Sophia would take my three daughters, Mimi, Brooklyn, and Amanda, as well as any nieces and nephews who happened to be visiting, to her house and play with them for days. She swam in the pool with them and, of course, she fed them. They had no idea how famous she was. Being around someone as family-oriented as Sophia was a wonderful thing for my family, and for me too.

All the time we lived as neighbors, I had the sense that she had her arm around me. And this friendship was a great embrace. She saw the real me and I saw the real her and we both loved what we saw. Having Sophia so close was like having another sister living down the road.

Sisterhood. Such a beautiful thing!

After several years of living in Thousand Oaks, Bruce and I agreed that the time had come to move again. This time we decided to move back to the East Coast. Bruce's family was mostly in New York and mine was in Boston. We decided on someplace midway between the two. Mimi was going to college in Connecticut, and I needed to be within driving distance of my younger sister Amy, who had been diagnosed with lung cancer. We wound up buying a beautiful contemporary house on Crystal Lake in Westport.

Amy lasted about eight months, and her passing was very hard for me to deal with. I'd never known how painful the loss of a sibling could be and how it puts you in touch with your own mortality. It took me a long time to come to terms with her pass-

My parents, Mary and Andrew Gaines.
Photo courtesy of the Sudano family archives

ing. Oddly enough, it would be another Amy who helped me through my grief. Amy Grant's song "Breath of Heaven" helped to soothe the pain whenever I felt like I couldn't take it another minute. It's amazing how notes and words can comfort you. Her song gave me such peace after a long time of grieving. It was the help I needed.

Once I had realigned myself spiritually, everything else came into focus, in better perspective, beginning with a renewed desire to return to performing. I was ready to get back into the music.

✳

The first thing I needed to do was to consolidate my catalog of music. I signed with Polygram (the label that had bought out Casablanca). My attorney, Gerry Rosenblatt, helped organize all my legal affairs. I started to gather new material and write new songs for the *Endless Summer* album, and then I went back out on the road to perform—selectively, this time, as opposed to relentlessly. I promised my family and myself that I would do only as many gigs as my accountant said was necessary, and not a single toot-toot or beep-beep more.

I limited my more extensive touring to the summertime, when my family could join me, and scattered the remaining dates throughout the rest of the year.

What was wonderful for me during this period was the realization that I could go back out on the road whenever I wanted to, without a new record, and I still had an audience that wanted to come hear me. Thank God! When I did perform, I always did their favorite songs, both my own and those of others, like Don Henley's "New York Minute." I added a gospel section to my show, as well, which rounded the set out quite nicely.

I honestly believe that if you are going to be a great singer, songwriter, or musician, you must at least be acquainted with pain. If you're not, your performance may not have the depth or honesty required to project what it is you're trying to say through your music. A lot of my biggest songs have been about pain, even if their arrangements were upbeat and worked against it. "She Works Hard for the Money," "On the Radio," "Last Dance," "Bad Girls," "Enough Is Enough"—the list goes on and on. Even when I listen to some of the great singer-songwriters of our day—such as Bruce Springsteen, Sting, James Taylor, or Bob Dylan—I'll hear raw pain. There is a voice inside the voice. That is what we, as singers, get in touch with when we sing our songs. It is also a part of our connection, and when it is real, organic, emotional, and spiritual to us, it becomes real, organic, emotional, and spiritual to our fans as well. The right song at the right moment, even an ostensibly "happy" one, performed by someone who is connected to his or her feelings, can bring a listener to tears.

I feel a sense of responsibility for that emotional connection, and from that I have learned how to better deal with my own issues through music. If I stay in touch with them, I stay in touch with myself.

As I've said before, there's always a danger on the part of the performer that the pain will be unbearable, which is why, I think, so many performers have substance-abuse problems. They don't really understand or know how to control the emptiness or the pain, and finally it overtakes them; that was a problem that took me decades to conquer. Through spiritual re-demption I was able to find emotional release and put my music into perspective.

14

Bringing Up Babies, and Parents, Too

To the rest of the world I may have been the Queen of Disco, but to my husband I was Adrian and to my children I was Mommy, and those were the only two titles I cared about. I wanted to be at home every morning when my children woke up and every evening when they went to bed. I wanted my girls to know themselves and to be in touch with their own creativity. Children are great teachers too, and they can even help parents grow, sometimes by growing up ahead of them.

When my children were little, I would ask them what they could see from where they were standing. "I see the cabinets. I see the drawers," they'd say. Then I'd take them and put them up on my shoulders. "What do you see now?" I'd ask.

"Wow, Mommy! I can see the top of the cabinets and out the windows . . ."

"You see," I'd tell them, "I can see more than you can. I'm someone you can trust because I'm bigger, older, and more ex-

Getting my star on Hollywood Boulevard with Dick Clark, Mayor Tom
Bradley, Nell Carter, Red Buttons, my parents, Bernice and George
Altschul, Brian Edwards, and many of my friends and relatives.
Photo courtesy of Brian Edwards's personal archive collection; copyright 1992

perienced. And my vision, both inner and physical, is meant to guide you safely into adulthood. If I've done my job correctly, you'll be able to make your own wise decisions and see things properly."

At the peak of my career I decided to shift my priorities to God and to my family. My willingness to invest in my career became subservient to my devotion to raise my children in an environment that would prepare them for the best possible lives they could have. As I've watched my three daughters growing into womanhood, I've been positive I made the right decision.

In all the time they lived at home, our three daughters were never a problem. They were academically inclined, incredibly conscientious young ladies. Every night I would put them to bed by either reading them a story or singing a melodic line to them, sometimes with words and other times . . . no words, just beautiful notes. I would ask them to listen to the music and tell me the story they heard in it. I was amazed and astonished by their imaginations. Kids are so free! I learned from them to look at life as if every day were a mystery and everything new. It's a unique quality that children possess.

Sometimes Bruce and I would create stories for them, especially when we had to travel. I would sit at a microphone and he would play some background music, and together we would make up stories. If we were away for a while, I'd put together several stories, so they had a new one for every bedtime we missed. In that way the kids still got to spend time every night with both Daddy and Mommy, and that made them feel safe, secure, and *loved* in our absence.

On the nights I was home, after I had put my children to bed, I'd leave the room for a while, and just when I thought they were falling asleep, during that early stage of sleep when they are so receptive, I'd lean over each of them and whisper in their ears, *"You are beautiful. . . . I love you. . . . You are so intelligent . . . so special. . . . You make good choices. . . . God loves you and has such wonderful plans for your life."* Everything I wanted my children to be I whispered into their ears. If one had a problem, I would reinforce her ability to overcome that problem. I would try to dispel her fear about it when she was awake and when she was asleep. If one of them was frightened about something, I would tell her there was nothing to be afraid of, that she was very brave and that she was not alone. I'd tell her that one day she could win a medal at the Olympics! If one had a test, I would tell her how well she was going to do. I always reminded them how unbelievably honored I was to have been chosen to be their mother, and I really am.

I saw the benefits of love and prayer in my children's lives. I didn't make negative comments about them, which is something so many parents do without realizing it. For instance, if one of them was being messy, I would never say, "Hey, you're such a slob!" Instead, I'd say, "Your room is messy, and you're such a neat person! It's your turn to clean up." I believe if you speak negatively to your children, you are imposing that negative trait *on* them. If you keep telling them what slobs they are, all you are really accomplishing is the reinforcement of the negative reality of that fact. You'll get slobs. I didn't want slobs.

I always preferred to help at home. I'd cook sometimes and

Cooking up my special spaghetti sauce in the kitchen with my longtime friend Holly Green. *Photo courtesy of the Green family*

be involved in the planning of a healthy cuisine, and I especially loved to bake bread and make homemade cakes and pizza from scratch and find new and interesting recipes.

Gardening continued to be one of my favorite home activities. I love to be surrounded by natural color, organic growth, *life*. I crave simplicity and love primitive living as a balance to all the pomp and circumstance. It puts me in a special place, and while it may have appeared to others that I was doing nothing when I gardened, I was actually involved in a very profound ritual, for it was in the garden that I communed with God on a daily basis. And we must remember that historically it all started in a garden, the Garden of Eden, I felt right at home . . . the Martha Stewart of Disco.

I would be cutting back plants, pruning them so they would bear more fruit, and suddenly I'd hear God say to me, *I am giving you this time to become more rooted. Many of the bad things that happen in life are due to spiritual rootlessness.* I heard that message loud and clear, and it made me even more devoted to the priorities I had set for myself.

At this point in time, I was working only sporadically, doing concerts in the summer and an occasional gig here and there. I was still constantly being asked to make appearances, to do concerts, to go on the road, but instead I wanted to put as much energy as I could into raising my children.

In 1988 the family spent the summer in London visiting friends while I recorded some new music. I wrote the lyrics to "This Time I Know It's for Real," with Mike Stock, Matt Aitken, and Pete Waterman, a music producing team that

Mummy and I chatting at Mimi's wedding two months before
Mummy passed away from pancreatic cancer.
Photo courtesy of the Sudano family archives

worked with some of the hottest acts coming out of England, including Kylie Minogue and Rick Astley. They were like a factory, mass-producing hit after hit all over the world. They had a great sound, and I was happy to be a part of it.

I had a great time, working on new music and socializing with the British polo set. Christina, my German friend from my *Hair* days, had since married the captain of Prince Charles's polo team. She invited us to see him play. It was great, and I became totally addicted to the sport. It was so much fun to watch my friend Stewart MacKenzie and Prince Charles play, not to mention hanging out at the parties afterward. I found the prince to be charming, extremely well mannered, down-to-earth, and a royal "dude." On one occasion Princess Di presented the trophy to the team that won. She looked so lovely. I'm glad to have seen her, if only for an instant, in one of her happier times. Bruce and our kids were with us that day, and it's a day they will always remember. It made me realize how difficult it is to keep your private life intact while your public life is under constant scrutiny.

In 1995, Bruce and I decided to move to Nashville, where the new music scene was happening. While I loved Connecticut, it was a difficult place for Bruce. He didn't have anyone to write with, and the hour-long drive into New York to record or see his friends became a real drain. We were both ready for change. It seems that we are always ready to move on after a few years in any one place. Maybe it's just the nature of our creative spirits to explore.

I had been to Nashville in the late eighties to record an

Rosa with the girls at Uncle Barry and Aunt Jackie's wedding, circa 1990.

Photo courtesy of Rosario Argueta

album with Keith Diamond, who'd written a lot of Billy Ocean's songs. Nashville had a vibrancy long missing from both New York and L.A., jump-started by lots of fresh, young new talent with lots of natural energy.

While I was recording in Nashville, Bruce met with many wonderful songwriters, and soon we were attending informal jam sessions with them. It was exhilarating. This is what had been missing in Connecticut—camaraderie and exchange with other musical people. Sometimes we'd go to composer Harlan Howard's or producer Tony Brown's house and there'd be a dozen or so writers there. Guitars would come out and everyone would sing and play. There was a tremendous sense of fellowship, community, and union. It was a wonderful experience for Bruce and for me too. Nashville is a very interesting town. It's more diverse than people think. We felt a new vitality and excitement coming over us in Nashville.

I wound up driving around with a real estate agent to see the lay of the land and loved what I saw. I had to take Bruce with me so he could see what I was raving about. The homes were beautiful, the people were nice, and the quality of life seemed to fit us well. And there was land, lots of land. We loved it: space . . . privacy. Soon we both agreed that when the time was right, we would move to Nashville.

Connecticut was a very beautiful setting, simple and tranquil. Of course, Rosa was there to run interference for us. I planned and planted two gardens on our two-acre spread. I had a great herb garden there; the basil grew up to my waist. But even though my garden was doing very well, my relationship

With my friend Alice Harris after receiving my honorary doctorate in fine arts from the University of Massachusetts.

Photo courtesy of the Harris family collection

with Bruce was under pressure. Bored because he had no one to write with, he began to battle depression and would stop talking to me for days on end. I tried to help him. Finally our friends Richie and Carmella Circell convinced us to go to counseling. Though we had tried it before, at this point, it was crucial. Bruce was in pain. I was in pain. We needed help. We could hide it from others but not from ourselves. It helped us immeasurably to get counseling. We realized that this environment was really hard on Bruce. It was time to give him some relief. So after several months of counseling we began to seriously pursue a home in Nashville.

The time had come to start practicing our southern accents.

*

Things happened quickly after that. Bruce and I went to Nashville and eventually chose a traditional house, on four and a half acres of land but still in the city. We had found a place that satisfied both of us: a house not too far from a great private school and close to the airport, which is something I'd sorely missed in Connecticut, where it took more than an hour and a half to get to the nearest international airport.

We sold our Connecticut house in the middle of a summer tour, which was good. For the girls, leaving Connecticut meant having to say good-bye to all their friends and the home they had grown to love. I explained to them that life was all about change and promised them that they would enjoy this new phase of their lives just as much as they had Connecticut. But it wasn't an easy transition.

Backstage with the girls after a show. Left to right: Samantha (Alice's daughter), me, Mary, and Alice. *Photo courtesy of the Harris family collection*

After we returned from Brazil we only had four days to pack up. But more importantly, we had to make a beeline to escort Mimi on her big walk down the aisle.

Since I'd known beforehand that I was going on the road, about two or three months earlier I had taken a meeting with a wedding planner. When I had done all that I could do, I gave the rest of the responsibility to Mimi and Bonna, her future mother-in-law.

It was a week of inspired madness. Packing, preparing, closing one house down, opening another one up. I spent those four days saying good-bye to Connecticut, and then we stopped off in Baltimore, where Mimi's wedding was held.

On June 24, 1995, Bruce and I tearfully escorted Mimi down the aisle into the arms of her new husband. My precious firstborn was breathtakingly beautiful. She seemed to float to the altar, fulfilling her childhood dream to become a blushing bride. The wedding was so beautiful, with fabulous floral arrangements, great food, and a rockin' band. Mimi serenaded her beloved as we tearfully watched. We danced with the in-laws and the outlaws, we sang, and we snapped up a ton of pictures of the two hundred family and friends that had come to celebrate with us. Franck, the crazy wedding planner from the movie *Father of the Bride,* would have been envious.

The day after the wedding we took an exasperated sigh and began the surreal journey to our new home. With the new configuration of our family, I soon discovered that Nashville was one of the few places I'd lived since returning from Germany where I felt totally at home. The house itself is typical Georgian,

At Mimi's wedding with a bunch of friends. Left to right: Mona Steel, who is now deceased; Alice Harris, the author of the books *The White T* and *The Blue Jean*; me; Ceil Kasha, interior decorator, friend, and fine arts manager; and Bernice, who has been like a mother to me for many years. *Photo courtesy of the Harris family collection*

with lovely grounds and wonderful little extras. Beyond that, I soon discovered that Nashvillians have a charming pervasive social and moral structure that is unusual in today's world.

Unfortunately, we were in our new house for only four days before I had to go back on the road, leaving the burden of unpacking to Rosa—poor Rosa, my domestic engineer and right hand. So off Bruce, the girls, and I went, to tour all summer.

As August rolled around, I was finding life on the road with Bruce, the girls, the band, and our road crew a ton of fun. We were so revved up. By the time we got to the West Coast, we were playing to sold-out shows, and our performances were really tight. Our show in L.A. at the Universal Amphitheatre was one of the best shows I have ever given. The audience was phenomenal, holding candles, crying, and hugging each other. There were no aisles left, just a mass of people. It was so moving that the musicians, including Bruce, had tears in their eyes. It seemed to be a prelude to what was about to come. We were all so happy to be there. It was the ultimate artist-audience experience of my career.

Afterward we took a few days off in between shows and made a quick trip home. No sooner had we arrived in Nashville than I received a call from my father, who was now living in Atlanta. "Donna, you need to come and see your mother immediately," he solemnly told me. We drove to Atlanta the next day.

Upon arrival, my father took me aside and said, "I need to tell you something. Your mother"—he paused, and a grave look came over his face—"has pancreatic cancer. It's incurable." I couldn't breathe. It felt as if I had been shot through the heart.

Brian Edwards, a friend, comedian, and former employee (and one of the people who helped in research for my literary debut), receives my latest Grammy. *Photo courtesy of Brian Edwards's personal archive collection*

He helped me sit down. I couldn't think or even say anything. Bruce, the girls, and I all started crying. I couldn't get a grip on what Daddy had just told me. Trying to understand the implications I asked, "I mean, I mean, are you saying Mummy is dying? Is that what you are saying, Daddy?" He nodded. "Why didn't somebody tell me?" I demanded. "I wouldn't have gone out on the road if I had known this. She said she was sick but they had given her five years. That's not true?" If a room could weigh a thousand pounds, in that moment that room did.

During that week we rushed Mummy to the hospital emergency room several times only to be sent home with the doctors' obligatory condolences. We were told there was nothing they could do. I was certainly no stranger to pain, but this time I surpassed my own threshold. I felt suspended in an emotional no-man's-land. I felt as if I were being held prisoner in some bizarre hellish nightmare that would only end in an even worse nightmare. One by one my family and friends arrived. All hunkered down, we were "waiting for Godot." We held prayer vigils, sang, and prayed. Just before Mummy's passing, my family gathered around her bed, as if to form a human bridge between this world and the next.

As Mummy ascended across that bridge, it was as if she blew her last breath to us as a farewell kiss, and with that kiss stepped into eternity and became a citizen of heaven. Weeping and wailing ensued.

Losing her grandmother sent Brooklyn into an emotional tailspin. This was a lot of change and adjustment for someone as sensitive as she is. Something everyone should try to teach their

Bruce and I at the surprise party in L.A. for his fiftieth birthday.
Photo courtesy of the Sudano family archives

children is how to adjust to change, and how to do it *quickly*. I devoted a lot of time helping her get used to her new world and helping her adjust to her feelings as well, all the while nursing my own broken heart. It was very difficult.

What's really important, I came to realize, is to create an environment of emotional stability for our children for their own safety and sanity. This was one of the most essential things Bruce and I tried to accomplish with our children, and I believe we did a good job.

I am blessed to be able to say that our three daughters all turned out beautifully—physically, intellectually, and spiritually. I was determined to teach them how to be as beautiful on the inside as they were on the outside, and not to let the advantage of their attractiveness shortchange their character or their integrity. These are the priceless dividends of life. In time our children grew into soaring eagles and left our nest. Because we had always been there for them, and given them everything we had inside of us, they all grew strong and righteous, their wings ready to take them gracefully into their own skies.

Today, Mimi is married to Rick, her husband of eight years, who is studying real estate. She is a vivacious, warm mother of two children. She's singing, producing, and writing great songs. She's also a terrific piano player and a visual artist. When her children get a little older, she hopes to return to music on a full-time basis. She and her family live on the East Coast, happy and productive. Mimi is our earth mother.

Brooklyn is a Ford model and is studying at the Lee Strasberg Theatre Institute. She is an absolutely beautiful woman

Me (second from left) with Jeanette; Daddy; my sisters Mary, Dara, and Linda; my cousin Pearl; and my brother Ricky at a family gathering in Boston, circa 1998. *Photo courtesy of the Sudano family archives*

both inside and out. She's got a strong voice and is becoming a great songwriter. She plays the guitar and is also a visual artist. She loves to bake and is great in the kitchen. Brooklyn is our perfectionist.

Amanda is in her last year at Vanderbilt, majoring in communications. She plays piano, a little guitar, and also has a great voice. (All of my children are musically inclined, thank God.) She's a very quick study and will probably go into music and film as well. Amanda is the baby of the family, but she is also the family psychologist as well as a computer whiz and, oh yeah, she's our comedian.

By the turn of the new century, only after all my daughters were old enough to face life on their own, I finally felt ready to return to music on a more committed basis. I began to look for new subjects to write and sing about, and a new form in which to express myself. Well, actually, that brought me right back to my musical roots—Broadway!

✳

I have always loved show tunes, including big, theatrical numbers from Rodgers and Hammerstein and, especially, Leonard Bernstein's *West Side Story*—the good, old-fashioned musicals I'd grown up on and whose music I'd thrived on since I was a child. Since the mid-eighties I had worked from time to time on my own musical, a dream project I've always wanted to do, but now I poured myself into it. As I said earlier, my mother was always my biggest fan, and her greatest desire for me was to write musicals.

Many times in the past, I'd performed for her my concept

Backstage with friends, family, and crew. Back row, left to right: production manager Scott Schneider, Mary, Paul Green, and me. Front row, left to right: Brooklyn, Denise Eppolito, Holly Green, Bruce, and Chelsey Green. *Photo courtesy of the Green family*

for the musical. I would play each character and put the whole show on for her, singing all the parts and explaining the intricate plots. Sometimes she would get lost, wondering what had happened to such and such a character, only to be surprised at how I would always be able to wrap everything up by the end of the second act. I brought her to tears with these shows, and she would put her arms around me and tell me that this was what I should be doing with my talent. After my mother passed away, her death became the catalyst for me to really get the material written down. I wanted to complete the show so she could see the fruits of my creative labor, even if she would be looking down from above, from the first row of the balcony.

I got together with Michael Omartian, with whom I'd written several songs and albums, including "She Works Hard for the Money," and asked him if he would help me write my musical. There was one song that was living inside of me I had to get out, "If There Is Music There." We sat down and started writing, and in the first two days we had three songs that we both felt were better than anything we had ever done before. This told us that we were headed in the right direction, and I felt that maybe Mummy was up there, asking God for some special favors. We continued writing, and the show just came out of us. At some point we enlarged our team and added Al Kasha and my husband, Bruce. The show has became one of my major projects.

The most important thing to me is that, no matter what I am currently working on, I know I am raising my output to a new level of artistic expression. I don't believe the myth that

Left to right: Mimi on July 4, two days before giving birth, with Amanda, Brooklyn, and me (top center). *Photo by Rick Dohler*

says once you do one thing well, you can't do another. As creatives we ask that you loose us from our past so that we may soar into the future. Let us go where we go, do what we do, and create whatever we create. Give us the freedom to be free.

It has been a long and exciting journey. Once again, the time has come for me to strap on my climbing boots. I have been down in the fertile valley for a long time with Bruce, raising my precious children and tending my spiritual gardens.

I am returning to music with the inner strength, wisdom, and courage to withstand whatever obstacles may come. God molds us into a cup from which others may drink. My cup is filled with many wonderful things; one of them is music.

As I began, I remain . . . an ordinary girl.

Acknowledgments and Credits

I want to thank God for all that He has given me in my life. Writing a book has long been a desire of mine. One of the most rewarding aspects of a project such as this is the realization that my life has not been lived alone. It has taken many people a lifetime of giving and assisting and helping to get me through the things you have read about in this book.

I have had several bright and shining guiding lights in my life, beginning with my mother, Mary Ellen Gaines, and my father, Andrew Gaines, who showed me through their own experiences and sacrifices what they expected of me as a person. I thank them for all they poured into me and all that I became because of their unfailing love.

I want to thank my husband, Bruce, whom I love dearly, and whose love, support, humor, and patience have always been so strong and dependable. He was an invaluable help to me in remembering and clarifying many of the things I wanted to say in this book. I thank him for all of that, for coping with diva fallout, and for being in my life. Bruce, you're my hero!

I want to thank my children, Mimi (and her husband, Rick), Brooklyn, and Amanda, and my two grandchildren, Vienna and Savanna. They have all helped me to blossom into the woman and mother I am today. I am honored to know each and every one of them.

I want to thank my brother, Ricky; my sisters Jeanette, Linda, Dara, and Mary, and my late sister, Amy; my cousins Pearl, Carrie, and Sheila; my aunts Mary, Rita, Barbara, Mabel, Ruby, and Eula; my uncles George, James, Clarence, Allen, Eddie, Farley, and Barnie; my grandparents Eula Gaines and Annie and William Davis; my in-laws Lou, Madge, Barry, and Jackie Sudano and Father Glenn Sudano; and Lynn and Albert D'Agostino, all of whom were there for me whenever I needed them throughout my life.

I want to thank Dr. Mary Ellen Strong for her emotional support and prayers.

I'd like to thank my friends and chosen family: Rosa Argueta and Cesar Palacios; Bernice and George Altschul; Ceil and Al Kasha; Alice and Stanley Harris; Denise Eppolito and Eddie Hokenson; Holly and Paul Green; Linda and Joe Esposito; Michael and Stormie Omartian; Deborah and David Duclon; Hoby and Myrna Cook; Terry and Susie Christian; Sand Dei and Don; Carmella and Richie Circell; Gina Delgado; Nellie Prestwood; Pat Naderhoff; Christine Ackah; Bertha Joffrion; Garry Kief; and Anita and Daro Blankenship.

Acknowledgments and Credits

I'd like to thank my spiritual counselors: Jack Hayford, Dick Mills, Tim and LeChelle Johnson, Rice Broocks, Kimble and Melinda Knight, and Linda and Dan Fessler.

I'd like to thank my creative and business partners, Giorgio Moroder, Pete Bellotte, Harold Faltermeyer, Norman Brokaw, David Geffen, Gerry Rosenblatt, Don Engel, Gary Kress, Carla Green, Stan Moress, Joyce Bogart, Marty Beck, Rob Heller, and the late Neil Bogart.

I just want to thank Brian Edwards, Casey Kasem, Gonzalo Venecia, Marc Zubatkin, Ana Martinez-Holler, Will McBride, Carl-Walter Holthoff, Judi Lesta, Ulf Baumhauckl, Dagmar, Helmuth Sommer, Chelsey Green, Bob Conti, Judi Lesta, Tom Gilliam, Catherine Hawkins, and Taihisha Grant for their assistance in collection and research for this book.

Writing songs is generally an easy task for someone like me; writing a book has been an entirely new and different experience. I would like to thank Marc Eliot for his assistance. It is not intended in any way to be a work of vanity. Rather, I have sought to share some part of my life with anyone who may benefit from my experiences.

I'd also like to thank my editor, Jonathan Karp at Random House, and Susan Weaving and Mel Berger at the William Morris Agency. Also at Random House, I'd like to thank Steve Messina, Mercedes Everett, Stacy Rockwood-Chen, Gina Centrello, Bruce Tracy, Jonathan Jao, and Todd Doughty.

Thanks to Dan Rembert and Robbin Schiff, who designed the jacket, and to the jacket photographer, Andrew Eccles, and the team that helped at the shoot: photo assistants Ken Schneiderman, Matt Nyez, Agusto Murrillo, and Mike Webb; assistant stylist Silvia Sitar; Alan Cutler for makeup; and Edward Tricomi and Gwen Bourhis for hair design.

I'd like to give special thanks and credit to three people—Kimberly Manz, Kirk Manz, and Susan Munao—who worked unceasingly on this book with utter love and conviction. I could not have done this without you.

And finally, I want to thank all my fans and friends unknown, for years of continued support, encouragement, and love. Thank you.

Donna Summer Discography

1975 *Love to Love You Baby* (Casablanca)

1976 *A Love Trilogy* (Casablanca)

1976 *Four Seasons of Love* (Casablanca)

1977 *The Deep* soundtrack (Casablanca)

1977 *I Remember Yesterday* (Casablanca)

1977 *Once upon a Time* (Casablanca)

1978 *Thank God It's Friday* soundtrack
       (Casablanca)

1978 *Live and More* (Casablanca)

1979 *Bad Girls* (Casablanca)

1979 *On the Radio* (Casablanca)

1979 *Foxes* soundtrack (Casablanca)

1980 *The Wanderer* (Geffen)

1982 *Donna Summer* (Geffen)

1983 *She Works Hard for the Money* (Mercury)

1984 *Cats without Claws* (Geffen)

Donna Summer Discography

1987 *All Systems Go* (Polygram)

1989 *Another Place and Time* (Atlantic–WEA
       International)

1991 *Mistaken Identity* (Atlantic–WEA
       International)

1994 *Endless Summer: Greatest Hits* (Mercury)

1994 *Christmas Spirit* (Polygram)

1996 *Daylight* soundtrack (Universal)

1999 *VH1 Presents: Live & More Encore!*
       (Epic–Sony)

2003 *The Journey: The Very Best of Donna
       Summer* (UTV/Mercury)

Driven by the Music

Information about Donna Summer's Artwork

The art of Donna Summer reveals the dramatic energy expressed in her music.

Her paintings have been described as "music for the eyes." An artist since her earliest youth, she freely reveals her talents visually in haunting, vibrant imagery. She considers herself an abstract expressionist.

Her works are intensely personal, with expressive, jazz-like rhythms referencing her musical persona. She has sold paintings to the most avid contemporary art collectors around the world.

Donna Summer's artwork is represented by:

Ceil Kasha
Donna Summer Enterprises
458 North Oakhurst Drive #102
Beverly Hills, California 90210
Tel. 310-860-0444/Fax 310-859-8719
E-mail: SummerArt1@aol.com

ABOUT THE AUTHORS

DONNA SUMMER is an internationally known singer-songwriter whose music has earned five Grammy Awards, three consecutive number one platinum albums (she is the only artist, male or female, ever to have accomplished this), eleven gold albums, four number one singles, two platinum singles, and twelve gold singles. Considered the voice that ignited the disco generation, she has been an enormously popular and enduring performer and recording artist for more than a quarter of a century. Her website is www.drivenbythemusic.com.

MARC ELIOT is the *New York Times* bestselling author or coauthor of several biographies and books about popular culture, including *Down Thunder Road: The Making of Bruce Springsteen,* Barry White's *Love Unlimited,* and Erin Brockovich's *Take It from Me.* He divides his time between New York and Los Angeles.